MY BOOK OF RUTH

RUTTH THELMA COOPER BRESLAUER BURG
MEMOIRS

1926-1937

When I try to recall my earliest memories, they are a jumble. I know that we lived in Chestnut Hill on Sidney Street in the house my parents purchased before they were married. It was between Germantown Avenue and the train station for the commuter trains to downtown Philadelphia. The station is clearer to me than the house we lived in. I have no recollection of the interior of the house.

Each of our orthodox Jewish families had a large Seder on both the first and second night of Passover. Each family wanted my parents to come to the first Seder and go to the other family for the second night. Mother said she resolved the issue by going to the hospital and giving birth to me. Both grandmothers were busy preparing for Passover. This was a big deal since it meant changing all dishes, cooking utensils, and flatware as well as lining all the shelves for them and doing all the special cooking for the holiday. Instead of doing this they had to rush to the hospital to see me. Uncle Abe always said he would not "go to heaven" because of me since he was so excited when he saw me he went out and had a big chocolate ice cream soda which of course was not "paseldik".

I remember that a "big girl" Elizabeth lived next door to us and she walked me to school when my mother could not. I do remember my father holding me in his arms during a thunderstorm and teaching me to count the seconds between the lightning and thunder as we looked out the window at the lightening while he reassured me that it was nothing to be afraid of. I have never been frightened by such storms since. The only other vivid memory that I have is that I was invited to visit the home of one of my first grade classmates to play with her. They lived in a large mansion not far from us. I vaguely recall it was a member of the Widener family, a wealthy old-line family of Philadelphia. I came home all excited about the fun we had playing in a large room filled with racks of guns that they used for hunting. Mother was horrified when she heard this and I was never allowed to go there again.

One of my earliest memories is first grade. I took lunch with me but, for some reason, had no one to eat with. Whether most classmates went home for lunch or for some other reason I cannot recall. I do remember that I had to cross Germantown Avenue to get home and there was no crossing guard at lunchtime. I remember that once my teacher had me eat with her but that was not repeated. I am certain she wanted to eat with the other teachers and get some respite from a bunch of first graders. One day I decided to walk home at lunch time and I remember meeting my mother wheeling a carriage with Vera as she walked down the street. She was quite upset to see me since it meant I had crossed Germantown Avenue (a very busy, wide street with streetcars and autos) on my own. I was ordered never, never to do that again. The school had what I recall was a long flight of steps and one day the wind was so strong I was blown down them but luckily was not hurt. I suspect that they were not as long as I remember them.

My sister, Vera Rubin, was born when I was two and a half. Over the years we became quite close and have stayed that way for all our lives. Vera became a world-renowned astronomer and received every conceivable honor except for the Nobel Prize. She was mentioned on many occasions in magazines and newspapers as a possible recipient and in all likelihood would have received it had she not been a woman. She holds honorary degrees from most major universities in the US and abroad, I had the pleasure of attending her receiving the Presidential Medal of Science from President Clinton in the Rose Garden of the White House. I am very proud of her, love her deeply and mourn the fact that she suffers from dementia and no longer recognizes her children or me. That is not to say that we always got along. We had disagreements and I remember angrily chasing her around the dining room table for some forgotten reason.

We moved to Uber Street near Oganze Avenue in Oak Lane shortly after my lunchtime episode. One reason was that mother was concerned I might repeat my solo walk home. I learned from Daddy's tapes that the main reason was the depression and that my parents could not keep up the mortgage payments on our house. They rented the house on Uber Street. Philip and Rose Applebaum, my mother's brother and his wife, lived down the street. We played with their daughter's Lucille and Florie who were our ages. I was shocked one day when my friend across the street said she would no longer play with me since I had "killed Jesus." I do not recall if we played together after that. I continued to enjoy school although I cannot remember the name of the elementary school I attended there. I do remember that in one test we were given we were asked as a final question to draw an elephant. I drew an oval with a trunk and 4 legs. No one else in the class attempted to draw an elephant so I was the only one who got an A for the test.

We lived on Uber Street during the depression until 1935. Daddy worked at home repairing irons and cutting jig saw puzzles in the basement. The puzzles were from magazine pictures that he pasted on wood. He put each puzzle in a dark blue shoebox and Mother counted the number of pieces and wrote the name of the puzzle and the number of pieces in white ink on the side of the box. The boxes were placed in the local drug store and people rented them for one penny a day. I assume the local owner allowed this and collected the money and gave it to mother when we brought new puzzles each week. I do not know whether they were placed in other locations.

Mother was an excellent seamstress. She had studied to be a hat designer and often designed our clothes. She made many dresses for Vera and me during the depression. It was always a thrill to go to South Street in Philadelphia to buy a dress for a very special occasion. South Street was filled with shops and carts from which clothes and accessories were sold. Mother was skilled in handiwork and would make tatting trimming or smocking for our dresses. She taught me to knit when I was about eight and my first pieces were clothes for my dolls. During World War II mother and I knit sweaters for the Red Cross to send overseas to the soldiers. We were considered quite skillful so were given many garments to correct when they arrived with mistakes. I remember many where one sleeve would be many inches longer than the other and we did a lot of ripping out and redoing of garments. Mother also taught me to needlepoint and I do a great deal of it even to this day. My family has asked me not to give them any more pillows and I must admit I have many in my closets. My major pieces include the needlepoint of Ruth that is on the cover of this book. I also have one of Moses for Moe. The largest one I have done is a 4x6 copy of one of the unicorn tapestries found in the Cluny is Paris.

While we were living in Oak Lane, Daddy asked us if we would like a dollhouse. I guess he was looking for something to do. We selected a colonial house from a magazine and he built it for us. It is still in the family. Vera's granddaughter, Elyra (Laura) Young has it and I hope that she keeps it in the family when she no longer has a place for it. It had a large number of windows (30-40?) and Bubba Cooper crocheted curtains for all of them. She did beautiful, elaborate crochet work (maybe that's where my love of doing needlepoint comes from.) I wish I had some of the pillows that she made. The front and back of the dollhouse could be lifted off, as could the one on the enclosed side porch. The kitchen had linoleum on the floor. Daddy made a duplicate of their bedroom set (in Birdseye Maple) for one of the bedrooms. He electrified the dollhouse and put ceiling lights in each room. There was a radio in the living room at Locust Street. The room was directly beneath our bedroom so Daddy ran wires to a model radio in the doll-house and we could listen to the radio in our bedroom. There was a switch so the radio could be heard in both rooms, or only in one of the rooms. I remember that we listened to the English coronation early one morning in our bedroom. Not many people had radios in their bedrooms in those days.

While we lived in Germantown and Oak Lane, on Sunday we would go visit all our grandparents. This meant that my father still had a car since we had to drive through the Wissahickon Valley Park to get to both houses. The Cooper's lived in West Philadelphia on Locust Street near 52th Street. It was a block from their stores. All the adults worked at the store—the Ideal Glove and Corset Shop. During this time Bubba (Matilda) Cooper, Uncle Abe, Aunt Fay and her daughter Thelma, and for a while Uncle Hy and Aunt Sadie all lived in the house. Aunt Faye and Thelma had moved back in with her parents after her husband deserted her when Thelma was 6 months old. It was because of this that Daddy told Vera and me that once we married and moved away we could never move home again. He said he would help us financially if we needed help but that it was too destructive to everyone to allow a married daughter and child to move home. He saw what it did to his parents. I am told when we arrived at the house everyone would line up to kiss Vera and me but that I would scoot by as quickly as I could to avoid the kisses. Zadda Cooper died when I was quite young. I have just a fleeting memory of Zadda (Max) Cooper standing in front of the store.

The Applebaum's lived in a three-story house at 1615 N. Park Avenue in downtown Philadelphia. Zadda (Jacob) Applebaum was a tailor who made custom made suits. Bubba (Pauline) Applebaum helped him. She would entertain us by letting us sew buttons on pieces of material in the shop that was on the third floor of their house. I have better memories of their house than of ours on Uber Street. They had a large dining room and one of the few memories I have of Zadda Applebaum (he died when I was about 10) was of his conducting the Seder. We children were bored to death since it was all in Hebrew and we either fell asleep or became quite noisy. The Seder excited us since we got all dressed up with new white Mary Jane shoes and fancy dresses for the event. Zadda was very fond of his grandchildren and I remember visiting when he came home from market and had a kitten peeping out of the grocery bag as a surprise for us. I also remember the carp swimming in their bathtub for Bubba Applebaum to make gefilte fish for Passover. They had a player piano that we loved to be able to play since it made such wonderful music. Bubba Applebaum's sister, Bertha Tapper, lived a block away and we often visited her. Some of the Tapper family still lives in Philadelphia but I have no contact with them.

It was not until I read Vera's biography that I learned we both had the same thoughts as we rode through the Wissahickon Valley Park on our way home from visiting the Coopers—how could the moon follow us all the way home. She followed up on this, as she became a famous astronomer. I merely wondered. I do remember her throwing a shoe out of the window when she was about 2 and my father having to stop the car on the Wissahickon drive and walk back to retrieve it.

Aunt Faye married Sigmund Myers in 1934 and they moved to Suffolk, VA, where he was an optometrist. He became the father Thelma never had. I remember waving goodbye to them and Thelma as they drove away from Locust St. They were to be married en route and at the last minute my father jumped into the car to drive down with them to make certain they did get married. I never discussed it with him but as I look back I wonder about his rationale.

After Faye and Thelma left, we moved to Locust Street.

It was the heart of the depression and I am certain the reason was economic. Mother worked in the store and did the cooking. There were four bedrooms on the second floor. Vera and I shared the front room and Bubba Cooper had a large room at the rear. My parents had a separate room next to ours and Abe had a room at the top of the stairs. In retrospect it was not an easy situation. While Vera and I never realized it at the time, we were constantly cautioned not to make any noise since we should not disturb Uncle Abe. We attended the elementary school on 52th Street. On my 9th birthday, during a race in the school yard conducted as part of our gym class, I tripped when my toe caught in a hole in the concrete and I fell and broke my two front teeth. I remember Mother's expression when they brought me home. She hurried with me to our dentist (and family friend) Dr. Green completely forgetting she had my birthday cake cooking in the oven. In those days the solution was to pull the nerves and let the teeth die. However, since we lived within walking distance of the University of Pennsylvania dental school, Dr. Green suggested we go there to see what could be done. I became the "guinea pig" for the school and they kept the teeth alive with bulky crowns on them until I was 21 and the teeth could be ground down and permanent crowns put on them. The crown material was not as strong as today so I have memories of the crowns breaking well into my 40s. It was always at the worst time (travelling for a trial as a judge, a major event, etc.) so Bob Decklebaum, my then current dentist, made a temporary crown I could put over the tooth pivot until a new crown could be made.

I have many memories of our time at Locust Street. Bubba Cooper loved her garden and there was a back yard deck with flower boxes with blooming petunias and large hydrangea bushes surrounding it. There were a number of children on the block and we played on the porches (cops and robbers was a favorite game). Both Vera and I were amazed when we took our father to his 60th reunion at the Univ. of PA and drove by the house to see the small set of steps leading to the porch. We both remembered them as wide and long. I guess everything is relative. School was fine and I did very well. I was a good student and enjoyed school and loved to read. I read adult books and, in retrospect, did not really understand everything I read. For example, I remember, in reading Jane Eyre, there is a statement that she had a cowl over her head, and for years I thought it was a hollowed out cow head that somehow she fitted over her head. We were still living at Locust Street when I started junior high school. It was a longer walk for me although I do not recall just where it was located. I do remember a warm day during Passover when, in walking home I was so thirsty I stopped at the local drug store for a drink of soda water. There was no charge in those days. It was not until after I drank it I remembered is was Pesach and I thought I would be stricken dead since it was not "pa-seldik". Pesach was very important in those days. I remember the frantic labor as dishes, cutlery and pots and pans were brought up from the basement and all shelves washed and covered with paper while dishes were changed. There were also two enormous crocks in which schav and beet borscht were made. There were far fewer foods available in those days—no milk, butter or other daily foods except fresh meat and vegetables. Goose fat, well salted, was used instead of butter. Until his death, Zadda Cooper made the wine in a barrel in the basement. There was also an old Victrola in the basement and we used to listen to wonderful old records.

We lived on Locust Street from late 1934 until 1937. Times were hard because of the depression but our parents worked hard to protect us from it. When Shirley Temple dolls became the rage, Daddy talked a storeowner where they were sold to give him some work so he could receive two 14-inch dolls instead of money. We loved those dolls. Daddy made trunks that would open so we could put the doll on one side. The other side had a place to hang clothes that Mother made for the dolls and drawers for accessories. The boxes were covered with gold wallpaper and were quite attractive. Daddy had various jobs during the depression. In his tapes he discusses them in great detail. We were really not that aware of them at the time. I do remember a visit to open house at the Philadelphia Navy Yard while he was working there. We climbed down into a submarine. It was dark and small and very different from the nuclear submarine to which I was "piped aboard" as a judge many years later.

There was a movie theater at the corner of Locust and 52nd Streets. I had my first "date" at age 10 going with a classmate at a movie there. I also remember seeing David Copperfield there with Vera. She became hysterical when David Copperfield was being whipped. I told her to duck down between the seats but that did not help and I had to take her home. I was quite angry since I wanted to see the rest of the movie.

We took piano lessons from an excellent pianist, Elizabeth Gitlin, about a mile away and Mother made a game of our walking to and from the lessons. On the way back she would buy one piece of pastry for Vera and me to share. It was not until many years later that I learned we walked because there was no money for trolley car fare. Also, Mother could only afford the one piece of pastry. She told me how her mouth would water as she watched us eat it while she insisted that she was not hungry and did not want any. Each year our teacher gave a recital where her pupils would perform and she would also play. We would get all dressed up for the event and after it was over we would celebrate by going to the nearby ice-cream parlor. We would order hot fudge sundaes and I remember furiously catching the hot fudge as it dripped down since I did not know to only pour a little at a time on the ice cream and poured it all on at once.

There was a shoe store across the street from the family store. One time they had a contest and the winner and runner up would receive a pair of Ked shoes (the popular sneakers of that day). The contest was to count the number of pieces of candy in a huge jar. Mother counted twice—one for me and one for Vera. She worked hard at it and our entries came in first and second. We each received a pair of Keds—quite a treat. (I do not remember who was first and who was second).

There was a kosher chicken market at 52nd and Market (about 5 blocks from the house). We would walk there and select our chicken, and then the schochet would take it to the rear and ritually kill and clean it. There were no super markets. The kosher meat market was around the corner from the house as was the local grocery store. Milk was delivered in bottles to the house. It was not homogenized so the cream rose to the top. It could be poured off and beat into whipped cream. Later when bottles were designed with a pinched-in place there was an implement (like a spoon with the spoon at right angles to the handle) that could be used to separate the cream out. Ice was delivered in large blocks and put into the refrigerator. A drip pan caught the water as the ice melted.

Our parents had good friends, Ella and Sam Green. Daddy had gone to college with Sam. They had one daughter, Margery. She was my age and we were good friends. I was a bridesmaid at her wedding and I wore her wedding gown when Max and I were married. The Green's lived several miles from us and at times we would walk over to visit them. My first concert was as a guest of Sam and Margery. The Philadelphia Orchestra had a children's concert and a parent could take two children so Sam invited me to go. Leopold Stokowski was the conductor and I remember the event in detail. They orchestra played the Saint-Saen double piano concerto "Carnival of the Animals" and Stokowski had borrowed animals from the local zoo for each of the sections. He brought out two lion cubs for that section, a pony for the horse section and penguins for one of the sections. The penguins got loose and were running all over the stage—under the two master grand pianos and could not be caught until the attendants used the 6-story high poles used to open the windows of the concert hall. We children loved it. Children in the orchestra were invited to come up and ride the pony. Since we were in the least expensive seats up in the high balcony we could not do that. It was a marvelous afternoon and a wonderful way to introduce children to musical performances.

Mother, Vera and I would visit Aunt Faye, Uncle Sigmund and Thelma in Suffolk, VA, during our summer vacations. At first they lived in an apartment and later in a lovely colonial style home. Daddy would come for short visits but would not stay with us the entire time. We children had a great time. We would make up shows—singing and dancing—and insist that our parents sit there and watch us perform. We thought we were great. I remember one performance where we danced around the living room singing "isle of Capri" holding flowers we had picked from bushes in the garden. Actually, Thelma was quite talented as an actress and performed in a number of shows in Norfolk over the years. She even is involved today, at age 90, as a director of amateur shows and loves it. On Wednesday afternoons and on Sundays Uncle Sigmund would drive us to Ocean View or Virginia Beach to swim, lie on the beach and/or walk on the boardwalk. We would also visit relatives in Norfolk. Bubba Cooper's brother had settled in Norfolk and his children, the Kruger's and Saunders, had quite a family there. To this day they often have family reunions and we are on the list even though we are not direct descendants. Sadie Kruger was really the matriarch of the family and we spent many happy times visiting with her and enjoying her food. The Saunders were the wealthier side of the family having been quite successful in the wholesale meat business. They would often brag to Daddy that they had much more money than he even though they did not have his college education. Since it was the depression, Uncle Sigmund was not always paid cash for his services as an optometrist and would extend credit to patients. Sometimes we would drive into the country with him and he would collect his fees in chickens and potatoes and vegetables. We thought this great fun. The Planter Peanut factory was in Suffolk and we were able to visit it several times. We enjoyed it thoroughly—especially the sample we received of chocolate covered peanuts. Uncle Sigmund's office was in a store similar to the optical shops of today. Next door was an antique shop and Aunt Faye purchased many lovely items from the owner. Mother also purchased a few pieces of crystal. I still have the tall gold and crystal vase that she got there. I fill it with pussy willows and feel good every time I look at it. We spent most of the summer in Suffolk and, shortly before school opened, Uncle Sigmund would drive us all back to Locust Street. We would drive through the night and I still remember our traditional stop near Richmond where we would get freshly buttered toast. While we did not realize it at the time, I suspect it was quite a relief to Mother to get away from the pressures of Locust Street.

Some years we would visit Aunt Helen Peiper when she rented a place for her family at Atlantic City. Despite every effort to prevent it I would always get terribly sunburned. I remember the discomfort I had as a result. My skin felt like leather and it hurt every time I moved. I also remember my skin ultimately peeling off in long pieces. The great milkshakes we had from the shop on the boardwalk and the fun jumping the waves made it all worth it. Mother said that when Vera and I were quite young they would also vacation at the beach. We were both still in the playpen. I would be covered with mosquito bites while Vera got none. They had to leave because of my bites. I have both problems of sunburn and bites to this day.

Through the efforts of an acquaintance Daddy got a job as supervisor of construction of a state mental institution being built in Selinsgrove, PA. In his tapes, put on disk by

Judy Young, he goes into detail about the political aspects about which he knew nothing until just before he quit. The job required him to be in Selinsgrove, 60 miles north of Harrisburg, PA. He would come home for weekends. There was a small college in the city and Daddy went door-to-door asking if anyone would rent their home for the summer. If you remember Pete, you know this was not something he would usually do, but he was desperate to have us and Mother spend the summer with him. He found a lovely home of a college professor that was rented to him on condition that we would take care of the family's dog, a small terrier by the name of Patsy. Of course he agreed and as soon as school ended in June 1937 we set off in the Studebaker Daddy had purchased for Selinsgrove. It was a lovely town and I have many memories of the summer there. The Studebaker was a four-passenger coupe with a small seat in the back and a toolbox that Vera loved to sit on. We had always wanted a rumble seat so Daddy found one in a junkyard that he used to convert the back trunk into a rumble seat by turning the trunk cover upside down.

We had lots of company that summer since it was a short train ride from Philadelphia to Harrisburg. Daddy would drive the 60 miles to Harrisburg each weekend and take one set of guests there to take the train back to Philadelphia and pick up the guests who would stay the following week. Daddy started to teach Mother to drive and she would practice driving on this trip until she had one scary incident and never drove again for the rest of her life. We had lots of fun with the rumble seat and one night when we drove to Sunbury (the closest big town near us) to go to the movies, people stopped and starred as we tumbled out of the small coupe and rumble seat. There were four adults (Aunt Rose very pregnant) and five teenage children. I do not know how we did it.

We had never been permitted pets at Locust Street so we made up for it that summer. We had a kitten, two rabbits, Patsy and a puppy Daddy brought home for us one day. The puppy had long, white hair so we called her Fluffy. When she matured she turned out to have terrier short hair and people would laugh as we called out for Fluffy to come to us. We grew vegetables in the garden and eating ripe tomatoes from the vine was a wonderful experience. We had lots of adventures with the pets. Patsy took a great liking to Mother and would not let Daddy get near her if he tried to hug or kiss her. The rabbits would get loose and start eating the vegetables in the neighbor's gardens. When we left, Vera and I took the rabbits to our next door neighbor and came home in tears since he thanked us profusely and said now he knew what they would have for

Thanksgiving dinner.

I took piano lessons at the college and learned a great deal. We had lots of visitors during the summer and since Bubba Applebaum was with us, Mother continued to keep Kosher. The nearest kosher meat market was in Scranton, PA, and every Tuesday Mother would send an order to him. Meat was brought to Sunbury once a week on Friday and the driver would put it on the bus to Selinsgrove. Vera and I would go stand on the corner of our street and the bus driver would give us our meat order that he had brought from Sunbury and we would give him ten cents for the transport. There were no freezers so meat was bought and used. I remember one Sunday when we had lots of guests. Dinner included a full size rib roast. Aunt Sadie was bringing it to the table and it slipped off the plate. Mother quickly scooper it up and rinsed it off and announced we would eat the second roast (which was the first one washed off).

Near the end of the summer, Daddy received two telegrams offering him jobs as an electrical engineer at the US Department of Agriculture and another US agency. Both were in Washington, DC. Daddy had graduated from the University of Pennsylvania as an electrical engineer. After graduation he worked for the Bell Telephone Company and that is where mother and he met. He was bored with the slowness of the job. After I was born ne considered going to medical school and was accepted with a one year deferment on the condition he spend the year studying Latin. Not liking the thought of doing this he went into the laundry supply business with Mother's brother, Phillip Applebaum. During the depression it became obvious it could no longer support two families so he gave the business to Uncle Phil. However, it took many years for him to obtain a full time job even though he was qualified as a Professional Engineer. So he was delighted to receive the two job offers. It was not until years later that Vera and I learned that Mother had made it clear to Daddy that she would not return to Locust Street to live. She was very unhappy there and was concerned for Daddy and us that it was not a good place for us to live. We left Selinsgrove and returned to Philadelphia looking like a bunch of gypsies. Items were tied all over the car and, since Bubba Applebaum spent the summer with us, there were five us and Fluffy inside the car. We left the cat with a neighbor (not the one to whom we gave the rabbits) and we returned with quite a load.

1937-1945

We returned to Locust Street and Daddy went to Washington to start his job at the Department of Agriculture. Daddy was very concerned that he might not pass the physical required for the federal appointment and urged Mother to stay at Locust Street with us until he passed the exam. She refused. As soon as he got settled in his job she went down to look for a place for us to live. They were astounded by the prices but were lucky to find an apartment near 16th and Columbia Roads at Mozart Place and Fuller Street. It was on the first floor and had good size living and dining rooms, a bedroom and a sunroom off of the bedroom. Vera and I shared the sun parlor and as the older I chose the window side of the double bed we shared. It was here that Vera began taking long exposure photos of stars. I admit I was often quite annoyed as she woke me crawling over me to take time photos of rotating stars.

The elementary school that Vera attended was just around the corner from the apartment and Powell Junior

High School where I attended was several blocks away across 16th Street. We enjoyed living there and made many friends. Meridian Hill Park was close by and I would meet classmates there to do "setting up" exercises in the morning before classes. Since the southern part of the park is literally a hill, it was beautifully designed with cascading water flowing. We could stand at the top of the cascade to watch the fireworks on July 4th. While in later years the park became a dangerous place, at the time we lived there it was quite safe and we children could use it without any problem.

In nice weather we would often walk with our parents down 16th Street to Lafayette Park outside the White House and then walk back via 14th Street. There was a large market at 14th and Park Road where we would often shop. I took piano lessons and music classes at the Washington College of Music located on Connecticut and Florida Avenues in one of the Victorian homes there. Since I did not have perfect pitch (Mother and Vera did) my classes in harmony and ear training were quite difficult but I managed to pass them and receive a graduation certificate from the college.

Mother's cousin Sylvia Cohen and her husband, Milton, were two of our first friends in Washington. She was an elementary school principal and Milton became our dentist. Through them we began to meet some Jewish families and I became friends with a group of girls my age who lived further north in Washington. Phyllis Homes and Carol Jarrett are friends to this day. Vera also became friendly with girls her age that lived up in the "third alphabet." Our parents decided that it might be good for us to move into larger quarters closer to where we were making these friends and we were all in favor of that. After looking at houses up along 16th and Rittenhouse Streets and deciding believe it or not, that is too far into the country, we moved to 517 Tuckerman Street. It was a small, semidetached house with 3 bedrooms and one bath upstairs. We lived there from 1940 until 1945. This area had a large number of Jewish families when we lived there. The Jewish butcher was on Georgia Avenue. Mother had stopped keeping kosher during the war since it was so hard to get kosher meat and the doctor had said I needed to have liver to eat. She would buy kosher meat when Bubba Applebaum would stay with us for various periods. I had lots of friends and the whole group of us would spend many hours together at someone's home or going to the movies on Kennedy Street.

I was in 9th grade when we moved to Tuckerman Street, so I continued at Powell Junior High School. I would often walk the 4 miles to or from school. When I started high school, it was a much shorter walk since Calvin Coolidge High School was at the corner of 5th and Tuckerman, a few doors from our house. My class was the first class that went through all 3 years at the school since it was brand new. Our class was composed of Jewish and Catholic students and the two groups, while friendly, did not really mix. I enjoyed school and was a good student. Mr. Chassey, our biology science teacher, selected a small group of students whom he taught how to use the projector to show movies. I was in the group and enjoyed it very much. Another member of the group was Irving Cooper. He was quite handsome and he and one my friends became quite a pair. We all mourned when he was killed as a soldier in the Pacific zone during WW II. He never got to be the doctor he hoped to be. His cousin David Cooper did go on to get his MD and we would often reminisce about Irv and other classmates who got killed during that war.

Vacations were always family events. On one of our first summer trips after we moved to Washington, we went to Niagara Falls. Aunt Eva, mother's youngest sister, came with us. On our way to the falls we stopped to visit friends in Selinsgrove. The neighbors to whom we had given our cat were concerned that we had come to get the cat but we calmed their fears and told them we had just stopped by to visit. The cat was now a huge, fat, lazy animal that could hardly move. On another trip we went to New England and enjoyed our first fresh lobster bake. We did not make any advance reservations and would stay at motels along the way when we felt it was time to stop each evening. One night Daddy and I went up to a nice looking motel and were shocked when we saw the sign in the office "No dogs or Jews allowed." Daddy immediately told the owner we were not interested. I remember his running after us as we drove away shouting that he had plenty of space and would give us a special, low rate.

These were happy years. I had many friends and there were many parties—often at our house as small as it was. Most of the parties were undated and while a few pairs existed, most of us were just friends. Parties were much tamer in those days. No smoking, no alcohol or drugs, just fun and dancing to music on records and enjoying each other's company. For my 16th birthday, Mother made a luncheon for girls only. It was a beautiful spring day and Aunt Eva, Lucille Applebaum and Margery Green came down from Philadelphia in lovely spring clothes. There was a 16-inch snowfall over night (at the end of March) and I still remember walking with them to take the streetcar to the train station wearing borrowed warm clothing. Margery had a pair of Mother's galoshes on. They were size 9 and her shoe size was 5. She walked out of them every step she took and had to pull each one out of the snow to put it on again before taking the next step. We were laughing hysterically.

We got around mostly by walking or taking streetcars or buses. Rarely did we go by car. On weekends Daddy would sometimes take the car out of the garage for us to take a drive into the country up Georgia Avenue to Rockville and back over what was Rockville Pike and Wisconsin Ave. When we went to Philadelphia, we would drive out New Hampshire Ave all in the country until we reached the Univ. of Maryland and Route 1. We would always check that the clocks on the tower at the Department of Agriculture were the same time on all sides. Daddy had designed the electrical controls to make all sides the same. Everyone said it could not be done but he did it. Daddy would often be the chauffeur for some of us girls to and from parties since he did not want us to walk late at night. Even when I went to college he would insist on meeting me at the bus when I would return from night classes.

In order to have Vera and me educated in Jewish history, Mother taught Sunday school for many years at B'nai Israel, a conservative congregation. She taught the very young children and they loved her. For many years, people would come up to Mother and tell her how they remembered her as their teacher. Since she was teaching we did not have to be members of the synagogue to go the classes there. Girls were not taught Hebrew in those days and I regret to this day that I do not know Hebrew. Learning languages is not one of my fortes so I have been unable to really learn it in my later years. Vera and I were both confirmed. We wore long white dresses for confirmation and carried deep red roses. It was quite an event. I continued for two years after confirmation and was certified to teach Jewish history. I did so for several years until I became too busy and had young children so could not continue to do it

I was at a movie with Phyllis and Carol on December 8, 1941, when the film was interrupted to announce the attack at Pearl Harbor. It is one of the events that you remember exactly where you were when you hear of it. While we were aware of the possibility of the US getting into the war, and saw the newsreels and heard the radio news about the war, it was quite a shock to all of us. Everything changed after that. We were at war and rationing became a way of life. It became closer to me after 1943 as many of my classmates enlisted or were drafted and a number of them did not survive. Daddy became a night watchman and would walk the neighborhood to make certain there were no lights showing from any house since the blackout was a way of life for all of us. We also got used to rationing and stamps to buy meat, sugar and other scarce food items.

School continued on its normal course and I began to consider where I would like to go to college. My first choice was Radcliffe. I was at the top of our class and had a good chance of being the valedictorian. At that time George Washington University gave a scholarship to the first in class of each white high school in DC so it was likely I would receive it. Specifically note that it was only to white high schools since segregation still existed in the national's capital. Washington was south of the Mason Dixon line so everything was segregated. This had been quite a shock to me when we moved to DC in 1937. Philadelphia was not segregated and I had classmates and friends of all colors, although I must admit most were white Jewish friends. It was shocking to see separate schools, separate pubic bathrooms restaurants, separate water fountains and requirements that black persons sit at the rear of the bus and street car. They could only sit in the balcony at movies. I had many arguments about it. I remember a discussion with my piano teacher and her mother where her mother asked me whether I would marry a black garbage man. I am still proud of my response to her when I told her I would not marry a white one either.

I had been saying I wanted to be a doctor since I had loudly announced it one night at a family event when I was 9 years old. Daddy was very concerned about my going away from Washington since there was constant talk of bombing or firing from the Atlantic Ocean by German submarines. He worried that "his little girl" would be out of contact if I were out of town. I knew that medical school would be quite a drain on my parents since Daddy's income as a government employee while at the upper level was far from enough for college and medical school without great sacrifice on their part. College loans were unknown. Therefore, a George Washington University scholarship with free tuition was not to be sneezed at. I did graduate first in the class at high school and accepted the full tuition scholarship from GW. In today's terms, $8 a semester hour (the cost at that time) was not great but it was large in relation to income at that time. Daddy was among the highest paid at $3,400 per year.

During all these years, I continued with my piano lessons and tried to practice at least two hours every day. I became quite an advanced pianist and often performed at school events. Some thought was given to my continuing on as a musician and applying to Curtis Institute. Luckily this was not pursued. I never would have made it as a pianist and would probably have ended up as a piano teacher. I had one student while in high school. She was the ten year old daughter of a friend and I was paid twenty-five cents for each lesson. In retrospect I was much too demanding of her but learned how to be complimentary and not too demanding. In later years I have always wanted a piano in our house even though I have not continued to practice. Unfortunately, somehow all my music was lost in various moves and, while I have replaced a little of it, I have not been able to replace it all. Bach, Beethoven and Rachmaninoff were favorites. To this day, Larry teases me when he hears me bang out the opening chords of Beethoven's Pathetique Sonata. I do it to relax when tense or angry although it is frustrating to be unable to have my fingers perform the way they used to.

In my senior year in high school I got a job at the Department of Agriculture (Daddy was no longer there) as a part time typist. Each Saturday I would go down there for 8 hours. In those days the Government worked 6 days a week. I was amazed when I retired many years later to see my application (handwritten by me) and my record while there included in my personnel file and added as part of my years of service. I worked there full time during the summer from high school before I started college. I also made money baby-sitting for some of our neighbors. I was paid the munificent sum of 25 cents per hour. I was shocked to hear what my children paid for baby sitters for our grandchildren. I thought what I paid when I used baby sitters was high at one dollar per hour.

Graduation was an interesting event. It was in the evening and in the middle of it there was an air raid alarm. Since the auditorium was internal, we continued. I gave the valedictorian address and Carol Brooks (Jarrett) also spoke. The "fun" was after it was over getting out of our gowns and finding our clothes in the dark in the gymnasium dressing room since that had windows and it had to be done in complete darkness

In the fall 1943 I matriculated at George Washington University. I lived at home and commuted by streetcar and bus to my classes. Many of my friends from Coolidge and Roosevelt High Schools also went there. I was on a full tuition scholarship but had to pay for my books. I had received a number of gifts when I graduated Coolidge. Aunt Sadie and Uncle Hy took me on a shopping trip to buy clothes for college. It was the first time I had several new outfits at once. Sylvia Cohen, Mother's cousin, urged me to go through sorority rushing. It was quite an experience and I became a pledge of Phi Sigma Sigma sorority. A number of my high school friends also pledged the sorority. I was elected president of the pledge class and at our initiation was awarded the outstanding pledge trophy. I used part of the money Uncle Abe had given me at graduation for my sorority expenses. We had a lot of fun as pledges. There were dances where we wore formal gowns and we had joint events with Phi Alpha Fraternity. Phi Sigma Sigma had been founded at Hunter College by a group of non-Jewish and Jewish women. Hunter College was also a city college and many of the young women who attended it had gone to high school together in New York City. The non-Jewish girls were shocked to discover that their Jewish friends were not eligible for the sororities on campus since in those days most of the sororities and fraternities had discriminatory clauses so that only white Christian students were eligible to join. Therefore, a group of women founded Phi Sigma Sigma in 1913 as a non-discriminatory sorority. At the time that we joined it, it was really considered a Jewish sorority and, at least at GW, at that time all its members were Jewish. That is no longer true today. Many of the members are of different races and religions. There were two other Jewish sororities at that time but they did not have chapters at GW. Phi

Alpha was the fraternity that had only Jewish members. Since most of the students commuted and lived at home, the major social activities centered on the sorority and fraternity. There was only one dormitory for women at the time. I always regretted that I lacked the experience of living away at college and it was for this reason that I was anxious for our children to do so. I think it is an important part of growing up and living independently. Like most of my friends, I lived at home and went from home to marriage, to having children and never had the opportunity of only having to be concerned about myself.

The pledges of all the sororities put on a show each year. Our pledge class was having trouble developing a program. Some of the active members helped us write a skit. This was permitted. Dorothy Wolf Linnowes was quite clever in writing skits and did one for us based on various Gilbert and Sullivan songs. It was quite a hit and we won first prize in the contest. For another performance Dorothy wrote words to a popular song of the day, "They're Either Too Young or Too Old." I remember most of the lyrics she wrote to this day.

Classes were great and there was a lot of homework so I kept very busy. While there was time for socializing and playing bridge in the Student Union most of my time was spent studying. I very stupidly (in retrospect) completed my undergraduate work in 2 ½ years by going to classes during the summer as well as the usual semesters and carrying a heavy schedule mostly of science classes requiring laboratory sessions as well as lectures. I was anxious to get on to medical school. I did well in my classes but the "C" I got in my logic class kept me from making Phi Beta Kappa. Our logic professor only gave a higher grade than C to the girls who sat in the front row with their dresses rising high and their legs crossed. I was unaware of this when I signed up for this class and refused to play that game. He also taught the second logic course that I took but disappeared in the middle of the semester and the President of the university took over the class. I received an A since he graded on a difference basis. We found out that the professor had made a hasty departure from the university when the husband of one of the front-row students was wounded and returned home to discover that his wife and the professor were having an affair. This was a no-no at that time.

I majored in chemistry and enjoyed it very much. The leading chemistry professor on campus did not teach any class. We later found out he and some others in the department were working on the nuclear bomb. I got a job as a typist for the chemistry department and earned $8 per month. One of my responsibilities was to type the chemistry exams and many of my pre-med friends (all male, of course) would try to get me to tell them what questions were to be asked. They were unsuccessful, of course. Because I was working in the chemistry office I had a key to the office and the labs. It was only because of this that I was able to complete all my lab work since some of my labs were at the same time because of my crazy effort to complete my undergraduate work quickly. June Cohen Pollack, also a chemistry major, and Gertrude Geiger, a pharmacy major, were in many of our classes and we became good friends. June was amazing in the labs and would get perfect results every time. Gertrude married Jack Geiger who was the older brother of Vera's best friend Molly. While I do not see either of them very often these days, in our younger days our husbands and we were good friends and socialized a lot together. Jack was my first adult doctor.

My pre-med advisor was my biology professor and he was very negative about my desire to be a doctor. I still remember when he came up to me as I was on a stool dissecting a cat in an advanced biology class, and asking me if I had filed my application for GW Medical School. I was shocked at his question since he had been so negative about my interest. Apparently, he changed his mind when he found that I was a good student in his classes. Since filing closed the next day, I rushed out to get an application and filed it in time. He had told me to put him down as one of my references and I did so. He also told me that he knew I was interested in anatomy and offered to paint my organs on me in body paint if I would come to his office. You can imagine how shocked I was by that and would never go anywhere near the floor that his office was on. He also bet me a milkshake that I would get into medical school. I immediately took him up on it. I came home one day after having my eyes dilated for an examination to make out that I had a letter from GW Medical School. Try as I might I could not read what it said. I held it in all directions and under all lights to no avail. I had to wait until Mother came home for her to learn that I had been admitted to the class beginning in September 1945. To say I was thrilled is an understatement. I was afraid to go tell my professor that I had been admitted so was delighted to see him in the Student Union one day. I rushed up to him and bought him a milkshake and that is the way I paid off that debt.

My friends were amazed at my interest in medicine. We were allowed to take our formaldehyde soaked cat home to study and I remember Charlotte Maletz Blumberg being horrified when I met her outside the library carrying the box reeking of formaldehyde. Bubba Cooper was also horrified when she learned I was working on it in the bedroom where she normally slept when visiting us and she insisted on sleeping somewhere else on that visit.

As graduation approached I was informed I lacked enough credits in the arts to graduate. I insisted that there was no way I could complete my chemistry and pre-med requirements and still take the art courses that they said I lacked. I won that dispute and was allowed to graduate with a BS in Chemistry with credits from my first semester at medical school.

College was during the war years and while we had dances and other social activities, they were very limited because most boys our age were in service. My boyfriend (I forget his name) was in the Europe Theater and I was quite worried since he was in the battle of the bulge and I did not hear from him for quite a while. One of the boys I had gone with while still in high school was in the Pacific. We corresponded and he sent me a grass skirt from one of the islands that I kept for many years. He asked his mother and sister to take me out since he was not there and I would go with them and his sister's husband to movies and once even to a wrestling match. When he returned home after the Victory over Japan (VJ Day), he asked me to marry him but I turned him down as politely as I could. One college classmate I dated was about 6'4". I was much thinner in those days (a size 8) and it felt very strange dancing with him since I looked at the middle of his tie when we were dancing. Jane Siegel Kirshner, a sorority sister of mine, was 5'9" and the only boys around who wanted to date her were shorter than she was. She used to complain that all the tall boys only wanted to date me. We laughed about it for many years.

There was much rejoicing on our victory in Europe (VE Day) and VJ Day. I happened to be in New York City on VJ Day and it was an exciting and marvelous experience. Everyone was celebrating.

During the summer of 1945, a sorority sister of mine, Phyllis Buxbaum, asked me if I would like to play bridge with a friend of hers, Max Breslauer, and his friend Bill Levi one evening. Phyllis was an excellent horsewoman and had met Max when they would exercise horses in Potomac for owners who did not have time to do so. They both were excellent riders and would ride and jump the horses every Sunday since that was the day they were not working. We had a pleasant evening and Max asked me for my phone number. He called me several days later and asked me to go out with him. I found him interesting and accepted. We started seeing a lot of each other. He was the buyer of linens for the Hecht Company and Bill Levi was a level higher. Both had come to the United States because of Hitler's anti-Semitism. Bill was from Austria and Max from Breslau, Germany. In 1931 when Hitler came to power Max's parents were sufficiently concerned that they took him to a school in Zugeberg, Switzerland. They were not sufficiently concerned to leave Germany themselves or to get any of their assets out of Germany. Ernst was a graduate engineer but had taken over running the family fur factory with his older brother, Hans. It was one of the largest in Europe and had been started by their father. They sold and supplied furs to stores all over Europe. The family had been quite wealthy but a lot of it disappeared in the post- WW I inflation in Germany. I was told that when their mother died they opened her safe in her bedroom where she kept a cash reserve of one million dollars but it had become worthless in the inflation. They still were wealthy when Hitler came to power. Max studied in Switzerland with very occasional trips back to Breslau. He saw his parents on frequent winter trips they made to Switzerland where they all skied together. They were all excellent skiers. After a few years, Max moved to school in Zurich so he could intern with a furrier who was one of his father's customers. The family wanted Max to learn how to work with furs since he was the only grandchild and it was intended that he would take over the business in the future. At that time they still believed they would survive Hitler's rule.

In 1937 Max's parents decided that things in Germany had become sufficiently difficult that Max should immigrate to the United States. He came to Washington, DC because the youngest Breslauer son, Walter, had emigrated here in 1928 and worked for the government. He was not married at that time. Max did not live with him but roomed in a house in Northwest DC. Max was to sail from England to the US but first went back to Breslau to say goodbye to friends and take clothing with him. While there was no way to get money out of Germany, he was able to take clothing and had sufficient underwear and handkerchiefs to last until his death in 1964. Max was so shocked to see anti-Semitic posters in Breslau that he tore some of them down and threw the scraps in the street. The next day this was the subject of discussion at home between his parents. He was horrified to learn they were willing to accept it and they were horrified to learn he had done it. They knew if this was discovered it would be quite serious. Ernst had obtained permission to go on a business trip to England as an excuse to see Max off. While they had not been scheduled to leave for several more days, they left that afternoon to get Max out of the country.

Max arrived in New York in late fall of 1937. He came to DC and got a job as a temporary stock boy at the Hecht Company for the Christmas rush. He was able to impress them so much that he was kept on as a permanent employee and worked up to become the youngest buyer at the department store at the time. He had graduated Gymnasium in Switzerland and had hoped to attend college. However, since he had to support himself, he worked instead. He became a US citizen and when the war broke out immediately enlisted in the Army. After his Army training he flunked his overseas physical because he had developed an aortic valve heart murmur. Despite his arguments with the doctors, he was given a disability discharge. He was furious about this and it did not incapacitate him at all. He was an active athlete and rode, played a hard game of tennis and enjoyed all sorts of sports so he felt the doctors had over-reacted.

1945-1965

I started medical School in September 1945. I was quite upset that classes started on Yom Kippur. The school would not change the starting date so I went and fasted for my first day of medical school. At that time the GW Medical School was in the 1300 block of H Street in an old four-story brick building next to the George Washington Hospital. Both buildings were quite old and sorely in need of replacement. That happened several years later and eventually the buildings were torn down and a more modern office building replaced them when the medical school moved to 23rd Street. Anatomy classes were on the fourth floor and it was quite a struggle to carry all our books and the box of bones up to class. We were not allowed to use the creaky elevator. The head of the anatomy department was a sadist. He would lock the door at 9 AM after leering at anyone still hurrying up the steps but not yet in the classroom. The locked-out students were not permitted to take the weekly exam. I suspect he was gay although I was too innocent to recognize it at the time. He taught gross anatomy and each week we had an exam that consisted of 6 questions, each worth 16 points so that the highest one could get was 96. Passing was 80 so if you missed one question you flunked the exam. Many questions allowed only a one-word answer and we could not explain our rationale. I still remember one question: Would it be better to sever the radial or ulna nerve in the arm. Since he had a master grand piano in the lecture hall (he had been the accompanist of a famous soprano), I answered the question correctly but many of my classmates did not. Each September he would move into the rooming house where a number of male first-year medical students were staying. He would not really socialize with them but they said he would creep around and spy on them. There were 10 women in our class. June Cohen Pollack was one of them. We were seated aphetically and all the women had to work on the same cadaver with no men allowed at our table.

He tried to flunk me out of school. He had a rule that, if you missed an exam you could not make it up unless you had a doctor's excuse. I was ill with the flu and had a high fever so missed a neuroanatomy exam. I specifically went to my doctor to get a written excuse even though I knew what I had. When I took it to the Assistant Professor who was teaching the course, the anatomy professor was in the office, grabbed it from me and said that there would no makeup. When I asked why since I had a medical excuse he repeated that there would be no makeup exam. Since there were only 3 exams in the course, a zero was pretty terrible. The Assistant Professor teaching the course and my classmates were as shocked as I. Our instructor and the lab assistant gave me the highest possible grades for lab work (well-deserved I might add) and I squeaked by with a C. The night this happened the professor overheard my classmates in the rooming house discussing this and cussing him out. They all flunked their next exam with him. One time when he was returning blue books to us he called out "Cooper" and I held out my hand. Then began one of the back-and-forth routines as I reached for it, he pulled it back, I reached for it, he pulled it back several times and then he blurted out, "I thought you were Cohen." So I guess he was anti-Semitic as well as anti-woman.

Max would walk over from Hecht's at 7th and F and we would have lunch nearly every day sitting in the park around the corner from the school. We would see each other on Sundays—our day off. Max gave up riding on Sundays so he could spend the day with me. After WWII, housing in DC became quite scarce. Houses were selling at a highly inflated price and there was a domino-like effect, as each person would buy a house because hers was sold. One could generally get a time extension on moving out when the house you were renting was sold. Our house on Tuckerman Street was put up for sale and our parents decided not to buy it. They had to hire a lawyer to get a time extension for having to move after it was sold to somebody else. Unfortunately, we were at the end of a long string of houses sold and owners waiting for possession so the judge would only give a very limited time extension. The father of one of Vera's friends was a big builder in DC and he was building a series of apartments in Southeast DC on Mississippi Avenue. People were lining up to get them. Vera's friend spoke to her father and he arranged for us to have a two-bedroom apartment in one of the units and we moved in in 1945. While it was new and modern it was a long ride by bus to downtown DC. But we were delighted to have it. Max moved from the house in Northwest and rented a room in a house not too far from our apartment so he would be nearer to us. We were very much in love and this was obvious when he gave up riding and moved to a less convenient location so we could see each other.

I was quite busy at school. I enjoyed biochemistry and

my other classes but the tension with my anatomy professor really was quite stressful. He slipped on the ice that winter and broke his arm quite badly. My classmates were well aware I was seeing Max and teased me that Max must have tripped him. They also did not ask me for a contribution to the fund to send him flowers since they were well aware of the situation.

Max had always wanted to be an accountant but could not afford to stop working. His hours were too erratic and his buying trips out of town too frequent for him to go to night school. He decided to leave Hecht's to go back to study accounting under the GI bill. This meant a cut in his salary. Max and I became engaged in spring 1946 and wanted to get married. The sex drive was very strong and pre-marital sex was a no-no in those days. Wanting to get married raised a problem about my medical school studies. Max was perfectly willing for me to continue on. However, I had not been entirely happy with my first year of medical school and the economics of the situation were grim. We did not expect any financial support from our parents. Max was working part time as a bookkeeper while going to school full time. In those days while married men went to medical school, married women did not. I, therefore, decided to request a leave of absence after completion of my first year of medical school and it was granted. After Daddy died, I found a letter in his files from GW Medical School saying that although they did not usually grant a leave of absence since I was an outstanding student they were doing so. It is interesting that the letter went to Daddy not to me. That would not happen today.

In the 1940's girls married at a much younger age than many of them do today. Unlike today, in those days "good girls" remained virgins until after they were married so sex was a major reason for wanting to marry. Many of my friends and family were getting married and I attended lots of wedding and was a bridesmaid or maid of honor at many of them. I remember being maid of honor at Margery Green's wedding in Philadelphia one Saturday night and then taking an all-night train to Norfolk to be a bridesmaid at our cousin, Thelma Meyers (Laderberg) wedding that Sunday. It was lots of fun.

My first real job after leaving medical school was at the Naval Research Laboratory. It was located not too far from our apartment. (I was still living at home.) While the position was in the library, I was not working as a librarian. The library was the storehouse for all the papers of the Manhattan Project (the development of the nuclear bomb). There were long rows of four drawer file cabinets housing the papers. Our job was to abstract and index each paper so the scientists could locate and use them.

We typed the information on legal size sheets of special paper with the thickness of index cards and lined into 3x5 cards. Erasures were made with a special pen of fine glass threads. They were quite painful when they became imbedded in your finger—as was often the case. After the page was filled and copied on a special mimeograph type machine, the page was cut into index cards and the cards were placed in a file under the subject-index we had selected from a list. The work was interesting insofar as the subject matter was concerned but the typing became somewhat boring. I also learned that indexing is quite subjective. Even though there is a list of subjects, it is up to the indexer to decide which should be used. To this day I try to imagine how an indexer would determine just what items should be listed.

The Manhattan Project had been highly classified. While many of the papers had been declassified some had not been. Before working on the project I had to have a security clearance and this was obtained for me. Each night the security guard would try to open each drawer in each file cabinet. If any drawer had not clicked shut we found a security violation notice on our superior's desk the next morning and were reprimanded. It made me very unhappy dealing with classified material and in later years when classified matters were involved in the cases before me as a judge I went go to great lengths to have the parties stipulate facts that would avoid classified information wherever possible. Otherwise the entire trial had to be held in a secure area and all classified material locked up every time we left the courtroom at lunch or in the evening. I remember shortly after I was appointed as a judge, entering a classified trial with a message since the messenger did not have a security clearance. The government attorney was horrified by my presence until we could assure him that I had a high security clearance so could come into the room.

I considered the job temporary since I was certain I would return to school. The only question was where. I had not been as happy with medical school as I thought I would be. I realize I had only had my freshman year but the thought of dealing with sick persons really troubled me. I know that one became accustomed to it but I was not certain that I really wanted to be a doctor. I struggled with this for several years.

Max and I were married on December 21, 1946. I had always dreamed of a large wedding—as most girls do. Daddy told us that his funds were limited. We could either use the money for a large wedding or to purchase furniture for our home. At first I thought we should use it for the wedding. Mother had recently had a hysterectomy and I saw how stressed she was with the planning of a large wedding. Because of that and the fact that we had no other funds for furniture, we decided to have a small wedding. We were married in a suite at the Statler Hotel. Our guest-list was quite limited. Vera was my attendant. I cannot remember who was best man. We invited one Aunt/Uncle from each side of my family—Aunt Eva (Mother's sister) and Uncle Abe (Daddy's brother). It was not until many years later that I learned my other aunts and uncles were hurt not to have been invited. Both Bubba Applebaum and Bubba Cooper were present. Lucille Applebaum Weber was my only other relative present. She was there as my bridesmaid. Max invited Ernst's two brothers, Hans and Walter, but they did not attend. Rabbi Siegel of B'nai Israel married us. After the ceremony we all had dinner in the dining room of the hotel. I wanted to wear a wedding gown and Margery Green Romberg lent me her gown. I had purchased a tube of mascara to use for the photographs. Neither Lucille nor I had ever really used much make-up and did not realize that the seal on the tube had to be removed. Lucille was helping me dress and could not get any mascara out of the tube. So she continued squeezing it harder and harder until she finally broke the seal and the mascara arched out of the tube because of the pressure and landed all down the train of the wedding gown. She has never forgotten it or forgiven herself to this day. I thought it was quite funny and began to laugh. Word spread that I was having hysterics. Aunt Eva came in and made big pleats in the train and basted them down to cover the dark black mascara so all went well. Max was still working part-time at the laundry, dry cleaning plant and their expert was able to clean the gown so there was no damage.

We chose our wedding date for when Max was on Christmas vacation from school and spent a long time discussing our honeymoon both as to cost and place. Our funds were quite limited. At first we had considered skiing but, when Max told me how stiff I would feel for several days after my first attempt at skiing, we quickly abandoned that idea. We decided on Miami Beach and went by overnight train in coach class since we could not afford Pullman. We stayed at a small hotel on Collins Avenue and had a marvelous time. Miami Beach was not as developed or busy as today and Lincoln Road was lots of fun. We returned, not to Washington, but to Philadelphia where Aunt Helen had arranged a large reception for us for family and friends. Unfortunately, I missed most of it since I developed the flu and had a high temperature but I am told it was a wonderful affair. Aunt Helen, although hurt at not having been invited to our wedding, did not hold it against us and had the reception.

Mother had been working part-time as a bookkeeper for the manager of our apartment complex. It was still very hard to rent apartments but the manager had promised us that she would have a one-bedroom apartment for us. She made good her promise and Max and I had our first apartment several buildings away from Mother and Daddy. Bill Levi had connections with a New York City wholesale furniture distributor and arranged for us to buy our furniture from them. In those days we made frequent trips to New York to visit Ernst and Trude, Max's parents. They lived in New York in an old brownstone off Central Park West. In those days it was a somewhat rundown neighborhood and rents were cheap. Today it is another story. They had the first floor of the house and we stayed there when we came to New York.

At this time Ernst and Trude each worked as a bookkeeper in a local company. Let me digress here to tell a little about Max's parents in Hitler Germany since I am uncertain how much of the story you actually know. In 1937, after Max had come to the United States, the Nazi's wanted the fur factory and the family home in Breslau (as a headquarters). It had been made into three apartments—one for Max's grandparents, one for Ernst and Trude and one for Hans (Ernst's older brother) and his wife Lisa. Ernst's parents were deceased and Ernst and Hans ran the factory. Hans and Ernst were given physicals. Ernst was healthy and, therefore, sent to Buchenwald. Hans (having intensely exercised beforehand) was suffering from heart failure so was not sent to the concentration camp. I am not certain how he avoided it but perhaps it was different than later on. In those days, one could sometimes get out of a concentration camp if one had a visa into another country. Ernst's younger brother, Walter, was living in Washington, DC. He had immigrated to the US in 1928 and had a high level job in the government. He was able to use his connections to get Ernst and Trude and Hans and Lisa visas into Luxemburg while waiting for visas to the United States. In order to get Ernst released from Buchenwald, Trude was told to go to a certain location and "sell" all her jewelry and other valuables (including a collection of the Meissen monkey orchestra). While the jewelry was in a safety deposit box, (I am told it was quite valuable having come from her mother-in-law) she was fairly sure the Nazi's had the inventory. She therefore did as told and sold all the items for a few cents on the dollar. After all, her husband's life was at stake. Ernst was released from the concentration camp a sick man having developed a heart condition and problems from frozen feet. He was in his 40's. He never would discuss the stay with me. I know he would wake up at night screaming from nightmares. The only hint I had of his experience was that he was completely turned-off from religion. He was a smoker and had apparently been severely "cussed out" by an orthodox Jew at the camp for smoking on the Sabbath.

Trude's father was a pharmacist and owned a building in downtown Breslau where his pharmacy was located. Trude had two sisters. They had both left Germany shortly after Hitler came to power. Elsa and her husband (who was not Jewish) had been part of the Bauhaus art group in Berlin. He was a famous architect and a socialist so they had to leave right away. They had gone to Israel where he designed Haifa. He remained city architect of Haifa until Israel became independent. He then was fired as city architect. I heard two stories for the reason. One was that it was because he was not Jewish even though it was argued that he we being treated just as Hitler treated the Jews. The other is that he had such a bad personality that they were anxious to get rid of him. He (Peter Rading) and Elsa went to England where he taught at Oxford so he must have been quite good. After his death, Elsa came to the United States so she could be near her sister. She lived in New York City but we saw her on a number of occasions until after Trude no longer recognized her in later years. I will get into that story later on. The older sister and her husband also went to Israel. Actually he left overnight and she followed later with some of their assets. This was shortly after Hitler came to power. They settled on a kibbutz and were no longer living when I made my first trip to Israel. Their daughter Miriam and her husband became friends and even visited us years later in West Yellowstone when on a trip to the United States. We met their children and in 2013, when we visited Israel with our daughter Joan and her husband Dolf and son Max. There was a family reunion where we met a number of descendants of several generations. When Trude left Germany in 1937 her mother was too old to travel and Trude left her in Breslau. She could never find out what happened to her. She advertised after the war and contacted many persons to try to see what happened. She did trace her to a concentration camp and it is probably just as well that she never learned all the details since it haunted her until she suffered from dementia in later years.

Ernst, Hans and their wives lived in Luxemburg for about a year until their visa numbers to the United States came up. They knew it would be soon so had reservations to sail on a ship due to sail from Bremen. The few possessions they had been allowed to take with them from Germany were on the dock in Bremen waiting loading. The US Consul in Luxemburg called them in to tell them their visas were there and that there was a ship sailing the next day. I do not know from where but not Bremen. Their ship was to sail several days later. Trude announced she could not possibly be ready to sail the next day. The consul told them that, even if he had to leave everything behind, he would be on the ship sailing the next day. Ernst was a bright man and got the message. They did sail the next day and were on the water for less than 8 hours when England declared war on Germany. The ship they were to have sailed on was bombed and sunk in the Bremen harbor along with all their belongings so they arrived in New York in fall 1938 with no possession except a few clothes and no belongings. Max hardly recognized his father when he met the ship in New York. He said that he had left his father a young, vigorous man and when he met him a year later he was an old, sick man.

In Luxemburg, Ernst had become friendly with the owner of a fur and leather plant. The owner had connections in the United States and arranged for Ernst to have a job in Gloversville, New York, when he arrived in the US. Ernst and Trude went to Gloversville but Ernst learned that the job involved illegal activities that he refused to perform. When I first met Max he was amazed that I knew about Gloversville. I told him it was where my father had settled with his parents when he first came to the United States in 1908. Ernst and Trude returned to New York City. For a while Ernst sold fuller brushes door-to-door but then obtained a financial position at a small company. He ultimately became the treasurer of the company. Trude worked as a cook and housekeeper for a family outside of the city. She was an excellent cook and taught me how to make many German dishes.

I still remember how thrilled they were to finally be able to afford to move to a studio apartment in a new building in Queens. They furnished it with modern furniture. Ernst was a great lover of classical music and a major item in the apartment was their stereo equipment.

I have digressed to give a brief summary of Max's parents' experiences since I do not believe it is available elsewhere. Now, back to my experiences.

Max and I were busy settling into married life. We enjoyed our apartment. We painted it ourselves. We painted one long wall in the living room in a dark cherry red and the rest of the room in pale grey. We thought it quite striking. There were a number of young couples living in the complex and we made friends with a wonderful group of young professionals living there, some of whom I still see occasionally today. Many are no longer living. One couple our age, Judy and Bob Bor, moved into the unit across the hall from us. Judy always remembered how helpful mother was when they moved down from New York so that Bob could take a legal position at the Department of Agriculture. We still see Judy at times at Temple Sinai where she is quite active. Bob died several years ago.

Abe Pollin was a classmate of Max's and we became very friendly with Abe and his wife, Lila (both now deceased). We would often play bridge with them and Max and Abe spent many hours studying together. They became part of our weekly bridge group. It consisted mostly of the girls I had grown up with and their husbands—Phyllis and her then husband Melvin Rosenberg, Carol and Irwin Jarrett, Janet and Joe Kirschner The women would play bridge at one of our homes and the men would play bridge or poker at another one. All of us had very limited finances at this time. Once a month we would splurge and go to dinner together on a Sunday evening. While we would eat at an inexpensive restaurant, we all thought it was great.

I was still friendly with June Cohen from our college and med school days. One day June called me so see if she could bring a young man to meet us. June's father was

Jewish and her mother was Lutheran and June was raised as a Lutheran. Her friend, Herman Pollack, was Jewish and we were the only Jewish couple June knew. We liked Herm very much. He was in the State Department and a very intelligent man. June and Herm eventually married (June converted to Judaism) and we remained close friends. Herm died a number of years ago. June and I still are friends, although we do not see that much of each other anymore. I am godmother to one of their sons and we have many happy memories of times together. My college classmate, Charlotte Maletz, married Marvin Blumberg and we became good friends of the couple. Marvin had a large, new car—a Hudson, I believe. We spent a number of weekends with them at Rehoboth spending hours waiting for the ferry coming home since this was long before the Bay Bridge was built. At times we even would play bridge while waiting in line for the ferry. We would also play with them at our home. We remained friends for many years. Unfortunately, Charlotte died at an early age. I still miss her to this day.

Money was very, very tight. None of us would have thought of asking help from our parents. Max and I lived on his GI Bill payment of $110 a month and my salary of less than $3000 a year. Max continued to work part time while in school but that brought very little income. Our rent took most of our income. I would shop very carefully. I would buy meat on sale and carefully cut it into small portions that I would freeze for our meals. We did not have a car and would go everywhere by bus and streetcar. Once in a while we would borrow Daddy's car for a special outing. While money was very tight, we were quite happy and looked to our future.

Max graduated with a BS in Accounting and then our next problem arose. The employment marker was flooded with graduating veterans and it was extremely difficult to get a job. He filed many applications. Max wanted to work in a public accounting firm since he needed one year of that experience to sit for the CPA exam. We used all our contacts without success. One evening, when on our way to dinner at my parents, Max met Sam Cohen, a neighbor in their building. Sam was the managing partner in the Washington branch of a Baltimore firm, Burke, Landsberg and Gerber. Max had spoken to him previously but they had no openings at that time. He asked Max if he was still looking for a job and said that they were looking for a junior accountant and Max should come into the office the next day for an interview. We were quite excited and even more so when Max actually got the position. It was a great firm and we became quite friendly with a number of the persons there. The salary was very low since all firms were aware of the experience requirement for taking the CPA exam. The firm did give good bonuses—distributed at the annual holiday party. We looked forward to that and I still remember our disappointment when we learned that one was not eligible until working at the firm for at least a year, but that first holiday party was only about six months after Max began to work there. In later years we did much better.

Max and Abe Pollin began to study for the CPA exam. It was a difficult exam in DC in those days and only a small percentage passed. Max sat for the exam after completing his year of internship and we were delighted when he passed 3 of the 4 parts. He did not pass the easiest section. It was at the end of the second day and I really think he was worn out by that time. He passed it easily six months later and was finally a certified public accountant.

After Max graduated and had a full time job I began to plan to return to school. I had always known that I would do so. It was just a question of when and what. I spent two years worrying about whether to return to medical school. Max was supportive of my doing whatever I wanted but felt it should be my decision. I had not been thrilled with medical school and, since we wanted to have children, I found the thought of 3 more years of school, then internship and residency somewhat overwhelming.

Max was nine years older than I so that meant he would be over 40 by the time I finished. It was different than it is today. Women did not become pregnant while an intern or resident. I had really liked biochemistry and, had there been a better school in DC where I could get a graduate degree, I might have done so. But, there was not. I had always said that if I could not go to medical school I would go to law school, so I considered that option. Since I had already been unhappy with my med school decision, I decided to take a series of aptitude tests before making a final decision. I found that one of the professors at George Washington University gave private exams for a reasonable fee and I made arrangements to take them with her. I realized that one could influence results with the answers one gave to questions but hoped the results would help me make my decision. Interestingly, law came out at the top followed closely by science and medicine. The lowest ranked career (rating a "D") was being a housekeeper—not surprising since I hated it and had hired someone to clean the house as soon as I could afford it.

I applied to George Washington University Law School and was accepted. In those days there was not much choice if one was limited as I was to the DC area, since the only other top law school, Georgetown, did not accept women. Since GW had night classes I decided to start at night school and keep my full time job, in case I found I did not like my choice—once burned twice shy. I had learned to drive (using Daddy's Pierce Arrow) and by this time we had our first car. Cars were difficult to obtain after the war but Max was eligible as a disabled veteran so we were able to get a Chevrolet. I still remember driving over to my parents the evening we got it and asking them if they wanted a ride. They thought we had borrowed a car and it took quite a bit of time to convince them it was ours. To get to my night classes in time, I had to drive from work. Max had carefully driven the route with me from Southeast DC over Pennsylvania Ave to GW. The first evening I did it myself, there was a fire that caused a detour from Pennsylvania Ave into what I found to be narrow streets. I was quite nervous and found it a terrible experience but I made class on time.

I enjoyed my classes, so I arranged to leave my job and became a full time student taking classes in summer school in 1948. In those days because of so many veterans in school under the GI Bill, many students went straight through including summers and completed law school in 2 ½ years. Since I was no longer working, money was even tighter than it had been. Max was earning more but school was expensive. We refused to ask my parents for help. For many years (until we got rid my mother's cedar chest) I kept the dress Max had gone out and bought for me to wear to a party we were going to. I had no dress to wear and felt we could not afford it but he went to a friend he still knew at Hecht's and she helped him select one that was lovely. It cost $8.00 (a large sum in those days). There was only one scholarship at the law school and it had not been awarded to anyone for many years. Today there are many scholarships and financial aid but in those days such help did not exist. I applied for the scholarship but again it was not awarded. Several of my professors learned of my indexing experience (maybe from my application) and asked me to index textbooks they were writing. I was paid the great sum of $1.00 per hour and this helped supplement our income. I will not go into great detail here of my law school and professional experience since it is all on the Oral History that has been made about me by the Commission on Women of the American Bar Association. It is housed at the Library of Congress and I have several copies on disk. If I ever finish this, I might incorporate it or add it as an appendix.

At the suggestion of Professor Fryer (I had indexed the Benson and Fryer text book on real estate law), I again applied for the one law school scholarship and this time I was awarded it. It covered my tuition for the final two years of law school and was quite welcome. I still had to pay for my books, which was a very expensive. When I first stated law school we still lived in Southeast Washington. Abe Pollin had a cousin (also Abe Pollin) who was a successful builder and real estate owner. He later became very successful and a leader in DC. Through Lila and Abe's efforts, we were able to get an apartment at 9th and Longfellow Streets in Northwest DC and we moved there. It was a far different neighborhood than it is today. DC was still a segregated city and it was a white, Jewish neighborhood. We were delighted to be closer to our friends and enjoyed living there.

I enjoyed law school. Studying was hard. A group of us would study together. Since very few places were air conditioned, we would study at the Jefferson Building of the Library of Congress, which had a conference room where you could sit and talk. Our class was quite large since we had many veterans. There were only about a dozen women in a class of 300. Many classmates were eager to study with me since I was getting A's in my courses. I still remember studying with a group of them before exams and being quite concerned since I thought that they knew much more than I did. However, I got the A's and they got B's and C's since most of our exams required written discussion of problems. I was the one who could reason from the precedents we had studied to apply them to the problems presented to us.

I would study in the law school library between classes and, since there was a lot of reading involved, I would often knit while reading the cases. Many of our friends were having children and by the time I graduated I had sufficient baby outfits to give as gifts for many years. My male classmates were startled to see me knitting away while studying.

I was asked to join a legal sorority and decided to do so since it was really the only women's network available. I was shocked when, in my senior year, while attending a meeting, one of our members reported that at the recent national convention, the motion to remove the discrimination clause from the sorority constitution had failed by one vote. Upon inquiring, I learned the clause limited membership to white women of Christian faith. While I was aware this existed in most undergraduate sororities it never occurred to me it would in professional sororities. I immediately tendered my resignation. The other members urged me not to do so since they were certain the constitution would be amended the next year saying that "you want others to fight for you." I agreed to wait to see what would happen. The next year again saw defeat of the revision and I immediately tendered my resignation. I learned several years later, after I graduated, I was claimed as a member when trying to get new students to join since I had graduated number one in my class. I wrote a strong letter to the chapter and to the national office telling them that, if this continued, I would bring legal action since I had resigned because of the discrimination clause. I never was claimed again.

As noted above, I graduated first in my class of 300. The Dean called me into his office shortly before graduation and told me that, while they normally obtained a judicial clerkship or an associate position with a leading law firm for their number one graduate, it would not be possible in my case since I was a woman. The most the school would offer was to write a letter of recommendation for any position that I could find. When I speak to young women today, I tell them I am less surprised that he said it than I am that I sat there and agreed with him. That was the situation then. At least that is no longer true today. While the school would do nothing to help me find a position, they recognized that I could be good publicity. At the award ceremony the day before graduation, I was asked to remain after the program was over and was interviewed and photographed with the Dean and the President of GWU. The picture was on page one of the local section of the two local newspapers the next day with a headline that I was the first woman to graduate first in class of GWU law school. There was a long article about me. I was so naïve that when asked by the reporter about my plans I told him I was going to take the summer off and then look for a job, but did not tell him no effort was made by GWU to help me get one. Looking back I am shocked that I failed to see what help the publicity would have given me.

One of the Phi Sigma Sigma alumnae, a practicing attorney, was angry about the failure of GWU to help me find a position. Her family had many political connections and she used them for me. Since I was interested in specializing in federal tax law, I was told to send my resume to three recently appointed judges at the United States Tax Court. I did so and one of them, Judge Stephen Rice, asked me to come in for an interview. I never heard from the other two. Judge Rice did ask me to clerk for him. We became quite friendly with him and his wife and Lee told me that, before he offered me the clerkship, he spent a number of days walking around their house muttering, "Never had a woman lawyer work for me before. She has a wonderful record." My record finally won out and I became the first woman to ever be a law clerk at the U. S.

Tax Court. In those days we were called Attorney Advisors not law clerks and some of the men stayed in their positions for many years. This was true of the two who had worked for Steve's predecessor, Judge Arnold, and when a judge retired his successor took them. When Steve offered me the position it was on the condition that he had a space for me. There were very few women judges at this time, and Judge Marian Harron was the only woman judge at the Tax Court. I am sorry to say that she had a reputation of being very difficult and, while she interviewed me, I was not anxious to work with her. Judge Arnold's two tax advisors were two of the most senior at the Court. Most of the clerks stayed only three years and then went on to other positions, as is usually the case with law clerks. Judge Harron asked for one of Judge Arnold's attorneys so Steve had the space and offered me the clerkship.

When I started working at the Court I found myself in a very awkward position. Not only was I the only woman among the 30 attorneys, but also Judge Harron had already decided she did not like Judge Arnold's former attorney and wanted him fired. He had been at the Court for many years and had two children in college so this was hard on him and I was immediately resented both for being a woman and for his problem even though I was not to blame. To make matters worse, there were two clerks in each private office and, since no one wanted to share his office with a woman, I was put in the office with Judge Harron's attorney. He was a lovely man and we got along but I felt very sorry for him because of his problem. We never discussed it. It was finally resolved when another judge offered him a position but the resentment against me by the other attorneys, not by him, never disappeared. I never was asked to join the others for their morning coffee break or for lunch.

Despite all this, I did enjoy my work. Steve and I became good friends and his senior secretary who had been at the Court for many years even finally accepted me. She had never worked for a woman attorney before and, at first, was quite resentful. When she realized I knew what I was doing and treated her well, she even began to like me. Steve rarely went out to lunch but after we finished a decision and had it ready for issuance he would suggest that we go to lunch together. As I said, I was quite naïve in those days, and it was not until many years later that I realized he was really an alcoholic. He had quite a capacity and his lunch was generally a bowl of vichyssoise soup and 10 or 11 double martinis. I had never drunk much alcohol and I learned how to make a few sips of one drink last during all of his drinks despite his urging me to have another. He had been legislative council of the Senate before appointment to the court and the other judges urged him to use his contacts to obtain their retirement system to be the same as that of federal district court judges. He invited me to join him for lunch several times when he had lunch at the Senate Office Building with old colleagues. It was quite a drinking event and while I found the lunches exciting I could in no way keep up with the alcohol consumption. They generally insisted that I have at least two drinks and, while I did not become drunk, this made me dreadfully ill. Max used to tease me about how would I feel if I came home and found him throwing up in the toilet! It was many years before I could face a martini again.

Steve and Lee had a house in Virginia built in the 18th century that had a beautiful circular driveway with lilac trees that were very old and very tall lining it. One spring when they came to our apartment for dinner he arrived with so many blooming lilacs that they filled our bathtub. They were gorgeous and the aroma was marvelous.

We were quite busy during the first years of our marriage between work, school and exams. Both Max and I loved music and had season tickets to the National Symphony, albeit in the last row of the balcony. Our first major purchase was a piano since I missed having one in our home. We found space for a full size upright in our apartment and I did find a little time to play. Our second major purchase was a radio phonograph combination. Sunday brunch included listening to Beethoven's 9th Symphony and over the years we wore out several recordings. We also enjoyed operettas and musical comedy. This was the period of outstanding musical shows and we managed to see most of them while visiting Max's parents in New York. They were great, even from the least expensive seats. One memorable trip to New York included getting a flat tire on the George Washington Bridge. Police immediately assisted us and offered us a choice of changing the tire for us or hauling us off the bridge. Luckily we had a good spare and it was strange to see our tire changed by armed policemen while one directed traffic around us. We also learned how much vibration there was on the bridge. They changed the tire in record time. On one trip to New York we met Vera and her husband Bob Rubin for dinner. A friend had recommended a steak house and, when we saw the menu, we all gulped. It was very expensive, considering our limited budgets, so we were uncertain whether we even had enough to cover the check. Vera and I suddenly announced we were not hungry and shared the cheapest thing on the menu making it possible for Max and Bob to each have a small steak. I think the waiter realized the situation. He was quite pleasant and gave us excellent service.

We remained friendly with Bill Levi and his wife Sylvia. They had much more money than we and lived in a lovely apartment on 16th Street, then a house in Georgetown. It was a small, converted and renovated carriage house and we would spend many peasant evenings in their garden during the hot summer months. Very few places were air conditioned in those days. They had a dachshund, Waldi. He was a very friendly dog and we got to love him. Bill Levi got a very top job in a New York City Department store and urged Max to join him there in a very good position. However, we decided to remain in Washington. They could not take Waldi with them and asked if we would like to have him. We were delighted to do so and he became an important part of our life. Max spent many hours training him in a class given by the city. He was quite intelligent and when Max entered him in a contest we learned he did not win because he had learned to do commands with hand signals that Max would use without realizing he was doing so as he started to give vocal commands.

I clerked at the Tax Court for about three years and then felt it was time to move on. I could not find a job other than as a legal secretary despite my experience so I decided to start my own practice. Before this Max had left Burke, Landsberg and Gerber and started his own practice as a CPA. I do not recall the reason he decided to do this but remember many hours of discussion before he did so. He shared office space with Jack Sheeskin and I used Max's office since I would not be evicted for failing to pay him rent.

Prior to this, we had bought out first house, a small three bedroom, one bath semi-detached house that cost $11,000. It was in Riggs Park, a post war development in Northeast Washington, There were several blocks of similar semi-detached houses and we had many friends who also lived there. Carol and Irv Jarrett's back yard was across from ours with an alley in between. With the assistance of the GI Bill we were able to make the down payment and get a mortgage. Flora and Arthur Feld and their three sons owned the attached house. Arty worked full time and went to law school at night. He became one of the leading negligence attorneys in the city. We became great friends. Unfortunately, Arty died while still fairly young while playing tennis one day. We remained friends with Flora over all these years.

Shortly after we married we joined Washington Hebrew Congregation as a way to become more involved in our community. We frequently attended Friday night services and would shake hands with Rabbi Gertenfeld after the service. Despite doing this for several years, it was obvious that he did not recognize us when we did so. We were not rich or important enough for him. When the congregation decided to move from 8th and G Streets, since most of the congregation had moved further north and into Maryland, they decided to build at Massachusetts Ave and Macomb Streets. In order to attend services members had to buy seats and the more you paid the further front your seats would be. The price was quite high. Many of us felt that we could not afford it, but did not want to go before a committee to plead poverty. At a meeting where this was discussed one of the young dentists we knew asked the president of the congregation what arrangements could be made for those of us who did not have parents who could buy seats for us, but did not want to plead poverty. The president was an attorney. I was aware he made or lost more in an evening poker game than many of us made in a year since his daughter-in-law was my law school classmate. He proposed a more liberal committee to whom we could explain we could not afford the seats. At that, a group of us stood up and left. While most were young professionals, one person who left was Irene Koenigsberger. She was my mentor (more about that later) and her husband's family had been long-time members of Washington Hebrew. Irene, and other long-time members, who could afford to buy seats, left the meeting with us. Together, we started a new reform congregation that we called Temple Sinai. One rule of the new congregation that has persisted to this day is that seats will never be sold at Temple Sinai. Max became comptroller of the congregation and was quite active in its governance until his death.

Max had also become quite active in Argo Lodge of B'nai B'rith. He knew of B'nai B'rith from Germany. He was elected president after serving in many committees and offices. Through these activities he served on the committee of the Jewish Community Center that was instrumental in moving it from 16th Street to Rockville, MD. I joined the Argo Ledge auxiliary for women. I ultimately helped found the Kroloff Chapter and become its first president. Irene Koenigsberger was very active in Jewish organizations, including B'nai B'rith Women. She became my mentor as I moved up the line. Irene was a remarkable woman. She matriculated at Hunter College, since she could not enroll in Columbia. She had a degree in chemistry, finally a PhD. During World War I she headed the artificial rubber program at the Bureau of Standards. She resigned after the war on a policy issue because she was a woman of strong beliefs. Her husband, Lawrence, was a DC Tax Court Judge. He died shortly after Irene and I became friends so we never really knew him. They lived in a large home on McKinley Street and their breakfast on Yom Kippur was an amazing event with lots of people and lots of food. They also had a lovely cabin off of Passage Creek near Front Royal, VA. It was on federal property and they had a 99-year lease. No one else ever built on the property but it was not isolated since it was on the trail to Signal Knob and hikers would often pass by. Max and I (and in later years all of our family) spent many wonderful weekends at the cabin with Irene.

I also became quite active in the Phi Sigma Sigma Alumna Association and became president about 1950. Attending national conventions, I became acquainted with many outstanding women senior to me who had remarkable achievements at a time when women had even more difficulty doing so than I. I was asked to run for national office and in 1955 became Grand Archon (President). As a national officer I visited many chapters throughout the United States and was thrilled to spend time with the undergraduates. They were remarkable women full of enthusiasm. I had my first transcontinental airplane ride when I went to Seattle and then on to San Francisco and Los Angeles. It was not my first airplane ride. One birthday Max had surprised me with Pullman train seats to New York and an airplane ride home. It was quite exciting.

Shortly after I started clerking at the Tax Court, Max and I decided it was time to start our family. Unfortunately, I had problems in doing so and had 12-14 miscarriages. Since many were quite early it was hard to know the exact number. I was unwilling to try drugs being used at the time since I knew enough to be concerned about long-term effects. I am glad of my caution since females born from women who had used these fertility drugs were found to have many serious problems. My doctors informed me that there would not be much likelihood of success from surgery, so we decided to try to adopt a baby. This was not easy as adoption was through religious agencies and the Jewish agency said it would be many years, if ever. We were advised to consider trying to find someone who did not want to go through an agency and preferred a private adoption. We let it be known that we were interested in a private adoption. Jack Sheeskin had a physician client who had a pregnant patient who felt she would not be able to keep her baby. We met her and agreed that we would be delighted to pay her medical bills and adopt the baby when it was born. In those days adoptions were completely anonymous and she wore a wig so we would not recognize her. We never knew her name, where she lived, or anything about her or the father. Unlike today, no medical history was available. On September 19, 1955, Jack called to tell us that she had given birth to a baby boy. I was in my office when the call came through. We had been on tenterhooks for weeks since we knew the time was getting close. To say we were excited is an understatement. I rushed out to buy clothes for the baby and I remember being with a friend and asking her what I should buy. To this day I do not remember whom it was I was with.

Two days later we drove to Baltimore (where the baby had been born) and the mother (again wearing a wig), in tears, personally delivered the baby to us. In those days, to have a legal private adoption there had to be personal delivery by the parent. We drove home quite excited and thrilled to bring our son home. Flora Feld came in to show me how to diaper the precious baby boy. Jack Sheeskin arrived with the necessary legal papers for us to sign without letting us see any names. This was how it was handled in those days. We never saw the documents and the court records were sealed so we never knew the names. I called Irene to ask her to be godmother and received permission from her to name him after her deceased husband. So with much excitement, love, and great joy, Lawrence Michael Breslauer (Larry) came into our lives. Words can never express our feelings. I spent that night until midnight standing at the kitchen phone calling family and friends to tell them the news. We had not told anyone before, so there was much excitement and joy when they heard the news. Mother and Daddy were in Ithaca visiting Bubba Cooper and when they learned they drove home at once. I am told that Pete did not take his foot off the accelerator the whole way home. Our friends living in Riggs Park rushed over to see Larry and give me advice on what to do. It was quite a change to be in an office one day and home with a baby the next. Larry was born right after Rosh Hashanah and his bris was to be on Yom Kippur. Flora Feld consulted her father, an orthodox rabbi, who said that the bris took precedence over Yom Kippur so it took place as scheduled. I do not know how many people attended the bris. I do know that our small house was wall-to-wall people. I remember Judge Rice who was over six feet tall, standing on tiptoe to watch the proceedings from near our door since he arrived later than many. Family came in from Philadelphia. Aunt Eva, whose business was to weave Jewish ceremonial items, quickly wove a tallit for Larry to be wrapped in at the bris. We still have it. It was a wonderful day.

Our lives changed completely and revolved about our

wonderful son. Mother would come over once a week or more if needed so I could do my legal work. Late night conversations at restaurants with persons active with us in Jewish organizations became a thing of the past. We remained active in our organizations and, if we both had to attend meetings, we took Larry in his carryall. Baby sitters for infants were unknown and even had they been available we would not have trusted our precious son to them. Friends could not believe seeing Max kneel down and coo and ah at Larry. Max learned how to change diapers and heat bottles and tenderly hold his son. Larry was a good baby and learned to sleep through the night quite early. We were a happy family.

Many friends told me that now I would become pregnant. This often happened after adopting a baby, but I would carefully explain that in my case it was not possible, and explained the medical reasons why this would not happen. How wrong I was. I attributed my fatigue to taking care of a baby and had no symptoms of pregnancy during the early months. I finally went to see my doctor and was embarrassed to tell him why I was there. He confirmed that I was pregnant and we were excited and delighted to learn it. My pregnancy was not an easy one. I spent many months off my feet. I was allowed to walk downstairs once a day and I wore out the upholstery on our sofa. The hardest thing was that I was not allowed to handle Larry. I sang to him, played with him but could not lift him, diaper him or carry him around. We could not afford full time help but our neighbors were wonderful in taking turns visiting with me and handling Larry. I spent most of my time either reading or watching baseball on our television. Mother came over two times a week to help out and Max took over when he came home each evening. I played more mahjong than you can imagine. I was allowed to go to my doctor once a month and we would celebrate with the most delicious roast beef sandwich after my visit. Finally, I was allowed more freedom when I reached my seventh month but then the doctor ordered me back to bed since he was afraid I would give birth too early.

Mother was not really fond of dogs. Unfortunately, Waldi our dachshund was very jealous of Larry. He never harmed Larry and would let Larry pull his ears and tail through the bars of his playpen, but Waldi showed it in other ways. When Mother would put Larry down, Waldi would jump into her lap and Mother would sit stiff and tense until Waldi decided to jump off. One day, when Mother finished diapering Larry, Waldi bit her. It was only a light nip but we realized we had to give Waldi away. We learned of an 11 year old girl who had had to have a mastectomy because of cancer and was very anxious to have a dog. We explained why we had to give Waldi up and she and her family thought that, since there was no baby in the house, they would try and see how things would go. Waldi was very happy there. We visited once but when Waldi saw us he immediately sat down next to Max and looked at him with soulful eyes. He responded to all the German commands Max had trained him. We never went back since we felt it was unfair to everyone, including Waldi.

Our daughter, Joan Marie, was born on December 8, 1956. When I Learned we had a daughter I was quite surprised since Dr. Gerber had always said it would be a boy. There were no tests in those days. When Joan was brought to me the nurses had tied a little pink ribbon in her large supply of dark hair. We were thrilled to now have a son and daughter and very grateful to Larry since we felt he was responsible for our having Joan. Dr. Gerber called when Joan was a week old to see how everything was going. When I asked him when I could handle Larry he said anytime I wanted. I rushed into Larry's room and grabbed him out of his crib. I will never forget the expression of surprise on his face. Mommy was someone who sang to him, and once in a while fed him when he was next to me in his playpen but never lifted him or carried him. I was thrilled to be able to do so, of course.

Life was wonderful but quite hectic. Having two babies 15 months apart was not easy. I learned to carry one on each hip. There were not double strollers as there are today. We could not afford a dryer and diaper service was quite expensive, so our basement was always full of drying diapers except on rare days when they could be hung outside to dry. Unlike Larry, who had been a very good infant, Joan was not an easy baby and would cry when put down to sleep. I have memories of rocking her to sleep in her carriage while sitting on the sofa. When I dropped off to sleep and my hand came off the carriage, her head would pop up and she would start howling again. Max tried to get me to let her cry it out but I could not. Daddy reminded me that I had done the same thing as a baby and he finally got me to go to sleep by keeping Mother in the living room until I cried myself to sleep while she cried downstairs. We went to Florida for a District 5 B'nai B'rith convention the June after Joan was born and Mother and Daddy took care of Larry and Joan. When we returned, Joan no longer cried when put down to sleep but went to sleep immediately. Mother had let her cry it out during the week we were away.

I still practiced law and life became quite complicated

as I juggled taking care of Larry and Joan and handling clients plus remaining active in my volunteer work with Jewish organizations. Our weekly bridge game with two tables of women friends was a respite from all of this. We looked forward to the day when at least one of our children would be out of diapers and decided that we would take a vacation when that occurred. Finally Larry outgrew diapers and we drove to Ithaca and Trumansburg to visit Aunt Sadie, Uncle Hy and Uncle Abe. We had a great time and they were thrilled to see Larry and Joan.

Max was still on the board of Temple Sinai. We did not yet have our permanent building, but had sufficient membership to hire our first full time rabbi, Balfour Brickner. His father was a well-known rabbi in Ohio and was a friend of Francis Sayre, Dean of the National Cathedral. He invited our rabbi to dinner and when he learned that we had outgrown our space, suggested we use the Bethlehem Chapel of the National Cathedral until we had a place of our own. We had Friday night services there until our building on Military Road was built. Joan was named there at a Friday night services and Aunt Eva wove a binder for our torah to commemorate the occasion. When we left we gave the National Cathedral a baptismal font for the Bethlehem Chapel and they gave us a stone from the Western Wall in Israel that is encased at the entrance of our temple.

Larry and Joan became the center of our lives and we spent many happy hours playing with them and watching them develop. Riggs Park was changing. Many of our friends had moved to larger homes and most of the homes were being sold to black families. We did not mind this and became one of the few white families living there.

Eventually we felt we needed more space and were quite concerned about the poor quality of schools available to residents of Riggs Park. We, therefore, began to look for a new home and decided to look in Maryland since their schools were much better than most of those in DC. We found a new home that we could afford adjacent to Kenwood Park. Kenwood Park was an area of expensive homes many of which were occupied by Jewish families. It was adjacent to Kenwood an area at that time which discriminated against Jewish and black families. Discriminatory clauses were still quite common in certain areas in DC, Maryland and Virginia. Our house was a split-level rambler with a full basement and three bedrooms upstairs. The basement also had a recreation room, a bedroom and bath. We had a large yard where Larry and Joan could play. Elementary, middle and high schools were all within walking distance. We moved into Westfield Drive in 1958. We had wonderful neighbors and became friendly with them. The Blemkers lived next door with their two sons and a daughter. They were about our children's ages and they became good friends with them.

About this time Max merged his accounting practice with Mel Oksner and Lloyd Welch. I continued to practice law and did most of it from home. For a short time I worked with Milton Baldinger, a tax attorney, but that proved not to be a good arrangement, so we parted company

We spent many happy weekends at Irene Koenigsberger's home near Front Royal. Irene also became a regular for Friday night dinner and really became an important part of our family. Max and I both remained quite active in B'nai B'rith and became officers in District 5 that included all the chapters between Maryland and Florida. Conventions each year were generally in Miami Beach since summer rates were quite low there and we would travel there by car enjoying sights along the way. Mother and Daddy would stay with Larry and Joan so we could get away. After tax season each year Max and I would try to get away for a week since this had been a very busy and stressful time. We often would drive slowly down the Blue Ridge Parkway stopping at interesting places each night.

Max always had his annual physical after tax season since he figured that was his most exhausted time. In 1961 he had his physical and this is when our lives changed forever. Dr. Dessoff informed us that Max's aortic valve heart murmur had become much worse since his prior physical a year earlier. He was surprised that Max had no symptoms such as shortness of breath or other symptoms indicating heart failure. He informed us of the major progress being made in surgery to replace the aortic valve. There were two places in Washington DC where it was being done—Georgetown Medical Center where Dr. Hufnagal had developed an artificial valve and the National Institutes of Health. We made an appointment to see Dr. Hufnagal who confirmed the diagnosis. He and his team were also surprised that Max had no physical discomfort because of his problem. Every time one of the doctors asked Max if he had difficulty climbing steps I had to laugh. We had just returned from our annual trip down the Skyline Drive where Max had stood behind me and pushed me up the mountains we were climbing. It was I not Max, who was out of breath. They recommended that Max undergo the surgery. We also explored going to NIH but decided to have the surgery at Georgetown. Dr. Hufnagal had developed a modification of the artificial valve he had developed so that it no longer made a clicking sound each time there was a beat. In October 1961 Max had open-heart surgery for replacement of the aortic valve. It was a long operation but when he was in the recovery room we were glad to receive the report that all had gone well. Our relief did not last long however. Several hours later we were informed that a problem had developed. There was bleeding that would not stop so they would have to take Max back into the operating room to see what could be done. He was awake but they would not let me see him.

This began what I always called "the night when the clock stood still." It was about 3 AM when a very tired Dr. Hufnagal came into the room and informed us that the bleeding had been resolved and that Max had survived. The room was filled with friends and family who had arrived during the evening and night as they learned of the situation. I was told later that there had been a call for whole blood for transfusions and that there was a long line of volunteers, all strangers, who had responded to the call. Bob Deckelbaum heard the call over the car radio and came down to be with me. Herm Pollack also arrived. We were very grateful to the strangers, including policemen, who responded. There are some wonderful people in this world.

Max did not recover well and spent about a month in the hospital with a low-grade fever. We remounted his excellent stamp collection together, as a way for us to spend the time. He was finally allowed to go home after he decorated his room with many signs saying, "Home for Thanksgiving". During all this time, my parents really took care of Larry and Joan. I spent most of my time at the hospital with Max when I was not involved with clients. I insulated Larry and Joan as much as possible from the situation and continued to do so until Max's death. In retrospect this might not have been the best way to handle it but they were so young I wanted to protect them.

Dr. Dessoff was not happy when Max visited him after his recovery. He felt that there was no improvement in Max's condition and that he might have been better off without the surgery. It was too late for that. We returned to our normal life and Max returned to full time work in his partnership, Oksner, Welch and Breslauer.

Once Max was fully recovered, we decided to take a trip to Europe. My parents offered to stay with Larry and Joan and we spent three wonderful weeks. We started in London and then flew to Paris where we rented a car. We drove through the Loire Valley and enjoyed the old castles. One day I saw a long line at a bakery so stood in it and had the most delicious brioche just out of the oven.

We then enjoyed our stay in Nice and had the most delicious bouillabaisse on a pier overlooking the Mediterranean. Irene had given us a gift to buy a souvenir, as a memory of our trip and in Nice we purchased the Baccarat candelabras that I still treasure. We entered Switzerland driving through heavy fog on the way up and I learned where the song to follow the yellow brick road must have come from. That is how we saw our path. As we passed the summit and started down the other side there was no fog and I can still visualize the beauty of the Alps against a clear blue sky. We pulled over and enjoyed the breath taking view. Tears rolled down Max's cheek as he sat there remembering his youth and all that had happened in his life.

My practice continued to grow and I rented downtown office space. I rented the rear door and two offices adjacent to the door from a large New York firm, Fried, Frank, Harris Schriver and Jacobsen. They had a large suite at Connecticut and K Streets with a back door as well as a fancy entrance. The rear entrance had a separate number and we put my name on that door. I had a separate phone number. I had an excellent secretary whose name I have forgotten. In those days secretaries took dictation and I would dictate my documents to her either in my office when Larry and Joan began attending school or over the telephone from home when Larry and Joan were napping or otherwise occupied. The law firm had no tax attorney in their DC office and there was some thought that I might eventually work my way into the firm. Many years later, when I was on the bench, this firm had, and still has, a major division involved in government contract law so I had many cases in which they appeared.

Max and I both remained very active in our community and in Jewish organizations. I also chaired a committee for the PTA and became involved with the Maryland Democratic Party. We developed many friends in the neighborhood through meeting our children's friends and through our organizational activities and also in our activities with Temple Sinai. We were a normal Jewish family. We had a series of dogs, including another dachshund, Pretzel and a beagle, Tyros. Tyros was a terror. He loved to run and managed to dig under our backyard fence on a number of occasions. He loved to escape from the house and run up to the school where he would run from classroom to classroom until he found Larry or Joan. I would get a call telling me "Your dog is here again! Come get him at once!!"

Max loved to drive in our series of convertibles. There were no seat belts in those days and we never had any concern about Larry and Joan sitting or jumping around on the back seat. Vacations with Larry and Joan were fun despite, at times, the usual sibling squabbles. One year we rented a cottage at Bethany Beach. In those days it was not as built up at today so we could watch them run and play without any crowds or concerns about their safety. Max remembered the sand castles he had built as a boy and had fun building them with Larry and Joan. I remember spending a long weekend at Atlantic City. Larry had been at a day camp that summer. I remember the lump in my throat as I put him on the bus to camp. One summer we went to Atlantic City for a week. Larry had just learned to swim and Max and Larry had races in the hotel swimming pool. We had adjoining ocean front rooms and we had given Larry and Joan strict instructions that they were not to come into our room until we opened the connecting door. They were quite obedient and did not do so. However, we had not thought to instruct them about the telephone and first thing in the morning the phone rang and Joan informed us that they were fighting. We did not know whether to laugh or be angry. It had not occurred to us that they would be sophisticated enough to know how to use the hotel phones that, in those days, did not have direct dial.

I remember driving home in fall 1963 and hearing the announcement that shots had been heard at President

Kennedy's motorcade. I visualized shots moving over the heads of people there and it was not until I arrived home that I learned that President Kennedy was dead. It was a shock for all of us. That night Max and I went to services at Temple Sinai, as did many of our congregants. It was quite spontaneous but it was more crowded than Yom Kippur services. I also stood along with many watching the funeral cortege go by on Pennsylvania Avenue. It was a sight I will always remember. I had seen President Roosevelt's funeral cortege many years earlier and found it quite moving. But this was even more so.

We had several happy, healthy years until early 1964. In January 1964 Max and I took a Caribbean cruise. In those days they departed from New York and we drove up and left our car to await our return. Unfortunately we had a nasty storm around Cape Hetaeras. I spent several days suffering from sea sickness. Max was one of the few persons on the ship who did not get seasick. Once I recovered it was a great trip. We visited a number of islands, made a number of new friends, danced, and ate too well although in those days I was still a size 8 so could do it. It was extremely cold when we landed and the wait for our car was exhausting, but we were glad we had taken the cruise.

Shortly after our return from the cruise, Max began to

not feel well. At first we attribute to the chill we had had while waiting for our car after our curse, but visits back to Georgetown disclosed that the replacement aortic valve was leaking. In those days there was no thought of a second operation to replace the deteriorating valve. It later turned out that, despite all the tests in animals, the synthetic value that had been developed at that time became quite spastic in the human body so that by the time of Max's death about 85% of the valves had failed. Max was told to limit his activities and go on a strict salt free diet. Again I tried to insulate Larry and Joan but, as Max became weaker, it was evident that he was ill. We did not discuss it nor did we explain the problem to the children. I did discuss it with their doctor, but he did not have any specific advice.

Max seemed well enough for us to take our second European trip that summer when Larry and Joan were in camp. We went to Scandinavia for three weeks and had a wonderful time. Mother said later that she realized we were doing all these things since we did not know how much time Max had left and she was right. I had arranged in advance for us to eat our meals at our hotels so Max could follow his salt free diet. The hotels were quite cooperative and our efforts were successful. Again we, really Max, drove through Scandinavia and saw wonderful sights. I remember a man spotting Max's B'nai B'rith lapel pin and stopping us to say how helpful B'nai B'rith had been during WW II. I made one goof when a man in Norway had trouble with our last name and I blurted out that it was a good German name. He froze and I realized my error considering how the Germans had abused the Norwegians during WW II and I quickly explained it was a Jewish name and he relaxed.

Shortly after our return to DC, Max became quite weak. I spoke to the doctors who said that they did not know what the prognosis was since he was one of the ones making the statistics. That caused some tears I can assure you. While Max's partners were sympathetic and there was disability insurance, one of them felt the partnership should be dissolved. Max was not able to go out, but he could work from home, and discussions were begun. Max went downhill very quickly. When I agreed to an autopsy, so much was going on that I never asked for or learned the results. I assume the valve was no longer functioning. This was the case for many of the Hufnagal valves used at that time.

On August 23, 1964 Joan was down the street playing with a friend. I handed Larry the mail for Max that had just been delivered and asked him to take it into Max. He did so and returned to tell me something. A few minutes later I heard gasps from the bedroom. I realized what I was hearing, told Larry to quickly run down to join Joan and rushed into the bedroom where Max had collapsed. I called for an ambulance, but realized it was probably futile. If I can be grateful for anything it is that Larry had left the bedroom before Mas collapsed. It was fitting that Max had opened a letter from B'nai B'rith District 5 about assuming an office in line since this had been such an important part of his life. The rescue squad took Max to the hospital although I think they did this to be kind to me since a doctor had not seen Max for several weeks and having him declared to have died in a hospital avoided some complications.

Trude was on vacation in New England. I had been shocked that she decided to go since Max was so ill, but it might have been denial on her part. My father did not tell her Max had died but that he was very ill. At first she was reluctant to return but agreed to do so only after my father had refused her request that he drive to New England to get her and insisted that she return. It might well be that her dementia was already developing.

The funeral was several days later. Family and friends came in from all over the country. I was not thinking clearly or should have had it at Temple Sinai. It was at Danzansky funeral home (the old one) and there was an overflowing crowd. I decided not to have Larry and Joan attend and I think Joan has never forgiven me for that. Again I was trying to shield the children and possibly this was a mistake. But I was trying to do what I thought was best. The procession to the King David cemetery was very long. I remember Rabbi Lipman exclaiming about its length as we rounded a corner and could look back. Considering it was in August and many people were on vacation, the attendance was much larger than I had anticipated. Max was a Mason, and Jack Sheeskin, who was quite active in the Masons, insisted that the Masonic procedure be included. Frankly, I was numb and did not care one-way or the other.

Shiva for seven days was at the house. No one discussed having services and I was too far out of it to remember. I have always regretted not having them. Considering I am not very observant today, I do not know why it bothers me but it does. The crowds coming each day and night were huge. I learned the therapeutic effect of Shiva. Having lots of people around and lots of conversation helps dull your senses. The grieving and crying come later. At least they did to me. I think it was helpful for Larry and Joan, also. They were busy visiting with people and accepting the piles of food that we had for weeks afterwards.

Then, we started to get back to normal or what would constitute our new normal. It was quite different. I was concerned about Larry and Joan since it is not easy to have a parent die. As difficult as it was for me it was much harder for them. Friends tried to help out and included them in activities with their children but it was not the same. Psychiatry was different at that time and grieving not as well understood. Rabbi Lipman was quite helpful and would counsel me. He even met with the children. I hope Max's death did not leave too major a scar on them.

Friends rallied round and tried to include me in various events but it was hard. Even though Max had been unable to go out much at the end, it was for such a short period that it had not had that much of an impact on our socializing. I was shocked by receiving phone calls from some of the husbands I knew who asked if I needed company and offered to come over. I immediately and unequivocally said no. I was also surprised at some of the wives with whom I was quite friendly who started to cut me. It was clear they did not trust their husbands. Others were wonderful and included me in a way that did not make me feel like a fifth wheel. Of course my sister Vera and her husband Bob were wonderful, but they were quite busy with their own busy careers and children.

My first concern was for Larry and Joan whom I loved

dearly and ached to have them in pain. I realized that I could not rely solely on my parents although my father did help with car-pooling quite frequently. I made arrangements for several Au Peres but frankly never obtained a good one so that was not too successful. One of my clients had died a week before Max, and his widow became very dependent on me. She really went to pieces, which set an example of what I should not allow myself to do or become. It really helped.

A major problem, and one that became worse and worse, was Max's mother. Her dementia was getting worse quite rapidly. One time I was called by the police after midnight and informed she was in their custody having been found in her nightgown on a bus in an unsafe area in DC. She told them she was on her way to the Hebrew Home where she worked as a volunteer. Larry and Joan were both in bed with fevers and I was beside myself what to do. I finally called on a neighbor who kindly came in to stay with them while I drove down to get Trude and take her to my home. She also became the victim of a woman in her apartment building that began to obtain money from her. A major concern was she had a key to our house and I feared that she might go there sometime when we were away and be ill or injure herself and no one would know. I finally called her sister in New York and asked her for help. Elsa came down, but when she saw Trude's mental condition, said that she would be willing to help her financially, but could not do anything else, and immediately left. I did not need financial help, just help to solve the problem. I called Walter Breslauer, Max's uncle. Walter and his wife, Tre, were living in New York and they came down. Tre was able to get my key from Trude and this was a big relief. With the help of some friends we were able to get Trude a space in the Hebrew Home. She was willing to move there, thinking she was going as a full time volunteer. She even made friends there, including a "boyfriend", until her condition became so bad that she was completely out of it. It was very sad but at least she was well taken care of. Mother was a volunteer at the Hebrew Home until they moved to Florida. She would feed Trude, who had reached a point where she did not speak or know anyone.

In December 1964 I took Larry and Joan to Miami Beach over the Christmas vacation. Vera and Bob and their children were visiting Bob's parents, so we spent most of the time together. We enjoyed the beach and Larry and Joan had diving lessons. It was good to get away. The day before we flew to Florida, I stopped in a Safeway to buy cookies for Joan's Brownie troop. As I was going to my car in the large parking lot, I noticed my wallet disappearing through the slit in the overcoat of a well-dressed man who had been behind me in line and was following me from the store. All I could think of was that my wallet contained the only photos I had of Max as a young boy. The others had all been lost when the family left Germany. One never knows how one will react in an emergency and, in retrospect my reaction was quite foolish. I turned to him and quietly told him to give me back my wallet. He did so and then insisted on taking my groceries and carrying them to our car. On the way to our car I lectured him on how such a well-dressed young man should be ashamed of such actions and could do better than stealing wallets. After putting the groceries in the car, he ran. I could not let Joan see how frightened I was but my foot shook so badly I could not put it on the accelerator. We were very lucky.

For a while I continued with my practice. However, when I found myself signaling to either Larry or Joan to be quiet if I was on the telephone with a client when they wanted something, I realized this could not continue. My practice had really become full time I was just doing it at strange times often when the children were asleep. However, at times I had calls that had to be handled when they were home and needed me. Luckily Max's partnership insurance and other insurance had left me in a financial situation where I did not have to continue my practice. While it would not be easy unless I had some supplemental income, I could manage. The children were far more important, so I decided to close my practice and did so early in 1965.

At about that time, Mary Bunting, Dean of Radcliff, was appointed an Atomic Energy Commissioner. A pet thesis of hers was the loss to the country because women in professions were unwilling or unable to work full time and she persuaded the AEC to start a part-time program for women. While most of the positions were for scientists, the General Counsel of AEC agreed to employ two women attorneys. Harold Green was a partner at Freed, Frank and had been responsible for arranging for my renting the space in that firm. I had met him when he was president of our PTA and he had convinced me to chair a committee. He had been an attorney at the AEC and knew Joseph Hennessey, the General Counsel. He suggested that Joe Hennessey consider me for one of the attorney positions. Since I was in the lucky positions of not really needing a job, I was quite independent and said I would certainly like to have it, if I could work at the Bethesda office, but not if I had to go out to Germantown. The Bethesda office was only a very short distance from our home and school so, if one of my children needed me (or if the school called that our current dog was running through the school looking for Larry or Joan—one of his favorite tricks along with the other one of digging under the fence) I could be home in a very short time. Paul Gantt, the Chairman of the Atomic Energy Board of Contract Appeals, had requested one of the positions. The Board was located in Bethesda and I became one of his legal assistants. I did not know there was such a legal specialty as public contract law. It is an arcane specialty and through the mentoring of Paul, I learned it and became a specialist in this area of the law. It framed my entire subsequent career.

It took a while for me to get the security clearance required by all employees of the AEC. This was fine since I had to wind down my practice, close my office and, most importantly, get myself back in shape emotionally. Uncle Abe wintered in Spain in those years and he invited me to fly over and spend several weeks with him in Madrid. Mother and Daddy offered to stay with Larry and Joan and they were willing for me to go, so I flew to Madrid via London. As we left London, a woman in the seat in front of mine released an emergency window thinking she was pulling down a shade. To say this caused some excitement is an understatement. It was too late to abort the take off so we took off as my neighbor and another gentleman jumped up and held the window in place. We landed after jettisoning all the fuel over the channel and, since there was no reserve plane available, waited for the plane to be repaired and taken up and tested. We were delayed for 6 hours while poor Uncle Abe waited at the airport for me. When we reboarded everyone took his or her original seats with the exception of the row in front of me where a large man was prominently sitting there while the woman who had released the window, sitting elsewhere, kept saying, "I didn't do it." As we flew down to Madrid I complimented my neighbor on his quick response. He said it was nothing compared with his experiences as an RAF pilot in WW I. I have forgotten his name but it turned out he was a retired Air Marshall of the RAF and had been in charge of the air part of the Normandy Invasion. He was a good friend of President Eisenhower and visited him when in USA. It was a beautiful, clear day and he pointed out all the Normandy invasion landmarks along the French coast. It was a fascinating flight.

I had a wonderful time in Spain. Uncle Abe was a very good host except that we ate in the same restaurant every night. It was a world-renowned restaurant but, still, it got a title boring. I returned much invigorated and ready to pick up my life. Since this is my life, I will not go into detail about Larry and Joan's lives other than how mine was involved with theirs. They can write their own memoirs someday. I would love to have the opportunity to read them (or maybe not).

I began my new law career and enjoyed it. Paul was quite a character. He spoke with a heavy Austrian accent so most people assumed he was born there. Actually he was born in Arizona but his parents returned to Austria when he was one year old. His father was chief of police of Vienna and was able to protect his mother from the Nazis even though she was Jewish. He was not able to protect Paul who used his US citizenship to return to the United States as a young man. He studied law at William and Mary and became a government lawyer and an expert on public procurement law. I learned a lot from him both about this area of the law and about how to function as a judge. The vice chairman of the board was John Roberts (not the John Roberts who became Chief Justice of the Supreme Court). Paul's official legal assistant was James Cohen. Jim and I became good friends and I learned a great deal from him, also. He was appointed to the Armed Services Board of Contract Appeals, the largest such board, and he later became Chairman of the Postal Services Board of Contract Appeals. We still enjoy each other's company when our paths cross. This is not often since Jim retired several years ago and moved out of town.

Paul had me sit in on the hearings and work on the opinions. He gave me a great deal of responsibility and during the seven years I was there I learned a great deal about procurement law. He also let me have great flexibility in my hours and he allowed me compensatory time for when I worked more than the 20 hours per week that my job required. Thus, I was able to fit my schedule to that of my children and not work when they were not in school. Whether this was exactly within government regulations I never knew, but no one complained.

I continued my activity in B'nai B'rith and stayed in line in District 5. In retrospect I did not do a good job after Max's death and should not have remained in office, but I really was still not completely recovered from Max's death. My social life was quite limited to events with family and friends, generally with our children. Friends tried to "match me up" with various men but I found most of my experiences distasteful and not worth repeating. Most of the eligible men were divorced and resented any positive discussion of prior marriage. I had 18 years of a very happy marriage and found it difficult to avoid discussion of things we had done or being positive about a prior spouse. Most men were only interested in sex. I was from a generation that considered sex something one did with a spouse and was not interested in getting into bed just for fun. I am not saying that this is better or worse than today's views, but it is the one that was part of me. I really preferred not dating but to spend my time home doing things I enjoyed or with my children or friends or family.

Larry and Joan went to camp for the summer in 1966. At their invitation, I accompanied Harryette and Bob Deckelbaum and Natalie and Melvin Clayman to a dental convention in Israel where their Jewish dental fraternity was presenting a clinic to Hadassah Hospital. It was a wonderful trip, the first to Israel for all of us. We extended it with a tour of Rome, Paris and London. While I had been to these cities previously, they had not. I remember letters from our children being delivered to us on a silver salver at the hotel in Paris. We had a great time and returned to DC refreshed and relaxed.

1966-1972

In fall 1966 Harriet Koven, a neighbor with whom I was quite friendly, said that a friend of a friend of hers had a widower friend whom they thought I would find interesting. She said that she was going to a dinner that the widower would attend and that she "would look him over." She reported back that he had been unable to attend since one of his children was ill and asked if she could give him my phone number on her friend's recommendation. This is how Dr. Maurice Burg and his children, Elizabeth (Betsy) and Robert (Bobby), entered our lives. I was called by Moe Burg and invited to attend a lecture at Beth El Synagogue. I do not remember the topic but do remember the evening. From my activities in Jewish organizations I knew many more of the attendees than Moe did, even though he and not I was the member of the congregation. He admitted afterward he never went to any events there but had been told of my interest and thought it might impress me. After the lecture we spent several hours discussing our lives, our children, our deceased spouses and our careers. This was quite refreshing after my experiences with persons who were reluctant to discuss their prior years.

Moe called me a short time later and invited me to picnic with him on Columbus Day while our children were in school. He brought the food and when he opened the container there was a beautiful rose on top of the food. We arranged for getting our children together so we could all get to know one another. We started to date frequently and also to include many occasions when the children could be with us. I realized that I was falling in love with Moe and becoming extremely fond of Betsy and Bobby. They were quite suspicious of me as were Larry and Joan of Moe. That was understandable. All of them had lost a parent they loved and were suspicious of a stranger coming into their lives. Lucy, the housekeeper Moe had hired after his wife's death, also entered our lives. Moe was very busy with his research at the Kidney and Electrolyte Laboratory at the National Institutes of Health. He had just recently developed a process for perfusion of kidney tubules that over the years made it possible to learn how the kidney made urine and what happened in the various segments of the kidney tubule.

Our relationship continued to develop. I had had a

happy marriage and was interested in remarrying both for the companionship and because I thought it would be good for Larry and Joan to have a father. Therefore, anyone I would marry also had to want to be a father to my children in every sense of the word. While I had become quite attached to Betsy and Bobby, I was not certain that Moe was interested in marriage or that Betsy and Bobby were willing to accept me.

Moe and his children spent the summer at the Mt Desert Biological Laboratory in Maine. I did not hear from him very often during the summer. I did have several phone calls and in the last call he casually stated that we should consider getting married. When he returned to Bethesda he did not repeat this and, after several weeks, we had a serious discussion where he told me, somewhat reluctantly, that he was not yet ready to commit to marriage. I think he was also concerned that I was five years his senior. Lucy told me later that when they spent the night in Newton Center on their way home from Maine she told Moe's mother, Augusta, that he intended to marry me. Augusta spent the night talking him out of it. She was concerned that, since I had children, I would not treat Betsy and Bobby appropriately. I was unwilling to continue as we had since I was too committed to him to date him and others and, as I had noted previously, I was interested in remarrying. I told him this and that I would stop seeing him. I did this reluctantly but felt I could not continue our relationship as it then existed. I could understand Moe's reluctance to make a full commitment. While he had loved his wife and felt committed to her, he had had a number of difficult years when she suffered from depression and was in and out of institutions until she ultimately committed suicide. Medications for depression that are available today were unknown at that time. During those years he had full responsibility for the children and for maintaining his household while doing his major research at NIH. It required a great deal of commitment to undertake the permanent responsibility, both emotional and financial, for an enlarged family. Moe was unaware of my financial independence. This had never been a subject of discussion. Our age difference and that he would be responsible for two additional children were serious issues that went far beyond our love for each other.

Frankly, I was devastated and missed not only Moe but also Betsy and Bobby. However, I felt that I had to get on with my life. I had had worse things in my life, and recovered from them, and hoped I would recover from this. I wanted to do something that would be exciting and help me go in a different direction. I was still involved with

B'nai B'rith. The six-day war was just over. Moe and I had worried about Chuck Greenblatt, a friend and colleague at NIH, who had been declared AWOL from the Public Health Service for going to Israel during that war.

I was invited to accompany a group from B'nai B'rith on a visit and briefing in Israel. Mother and Daddy agreed to stay with Larry and Joan so I agreed to go. Irene Koenigsberger was going and we arranged to room together. It was a fabulous trip. We were in Israel for Succoth and the celebrations in Jerusalem were remarkable. On Simchat Torah there was a ceremony at the Tower of David where the torahs that had been burned during the Holocaust were brought in from all over the world and carried in the service. Men (women were not allowed) danced with torahs through the streets of the Old City throughout the night. This was the first time all of Jerusalem had been a city as part of Israel since the second temple fell. No longer did we have to look at the Old City from the top of a building behind the barricades where we had to duck to avoid being shot at. We also toured up to the Golan Heights where the bunkers still contained blood stained clothing and the land still had active mines. One of the members of our group was on the board of the Israel Symphony and invited me to join him at a performance sitting in marvelous seats.

It was a marvelous and exciting trip. I came back completely refreshed and ready to get on with my life. I was invited to describe my experience on a Jewish hour program on television after my return. This was fun.

In early December I received a telephone call from Moe. I realized how much I had recovered since, at first, I did not recognize his voice. He said that he had found a jacket belonging to Joan in his coat closet and asked if he could bring it over. He arrived with the jacket in one hand and a large bouquet of flowers in the other. He told me afterward that he did not know whether I would invite him in or just take the jacket at the door and slam it in his face. I did the former and we agreed we would see each other for a short time to see how we felt about each other. Joan's birthday party was that weekend and Moe agreed to bring Betsy.

I had been unable to see the Sunday morning television showing of the interview of my trip to Israel. It had been taped earlier. A few days after Joan's birthday party NBC in Washington agreed to a private showing at their studio and Moe agreed to accompany me to the screening. Afterward we returned to my home and Moe formally proposed to me. I accepted. Since each of our children had a separate bedroom, we decided that, before we married, we should find a house sufficiently large for each ofthem to still have their own room. We felt that they would have enough adjustments to make and that sharing bedrooms should not be one of them. We hoped to marry in the spring. We started to look for houses but soon discovered that most homes that were sufficiently large were out of our price range.

I had inherited an interest in an apartment complex being built in DC and had also taken part of a legal fee in the same complex. In December I checked with Max's former partner about the income tax anticipated for this and other properties I had inherited as part of the partnership. Mel Oksner told me that there would be a substantial paper loss since a truck had gone through the garage cement in the complex and fallen through several floors requiring substantial reconstruction. There would be a sufficient loss to wipe out all the tax of my income and Moe's income for the year since at that time passive losses could be set off against earned income. We, therefore, decided to get married during 1965 and our wedding took place on December 30th. Thus our wedding date was set for tax purposes.

We were married in the library of Temple Sinai. Betsy and Joan were my attendants and Larry and Bobby were Moe's best men. Rabbi Eugene Lipman officiated. It was a small wedding. Our parents, and my mother's mother,

Bubba Applebaum, my sister Vera and her husband Bob were there. Early the morning of our wedding Moe called to tell me that his brother Jerry would be able to come since his wife, Harriyette, had given birth to their son, Geoffrey, during the night. My Aunt Helen and Uncle Abe were present. Unfortunately, Moe's Uncle Billy could not make it at the last minute since his wife Sarah was quite ill. After the ceremony we had a catered dinner at Vera and Bob's home nearby and then invited a few close friends to join us for the cake cutting.

The next morning Moe and I flew to St. John in the Caribbean for our honeymoon. We were lucky since we got out just ahead of a snowstorm that prevented out of town relatives from leaving for several days. Moe and I welcomed the New Year drinking champagne standing in the Caribbean and watching the fireworks going on around us. We were very much in love and grateful for a second chance. We had a wonderful honeymoon. One day we went out on a small sailboat and while away from shore I confessed to Moe that I did not swim and he confessed to me that he had never sailed. But we survived.

Since we had not yet found a home for our enlarged family, we settled in my house on Westfield Drive. This meant that the children had to share rooms and we felt that this could not continue. We kept Betsy and Bobby in their present school since we did not want them to change schools twice—once now and once when we found a house to move to. We worked hard to meld our families together. This was not an easy task. On the contrary, it was sheer hell and raised many second thoughts. The end of the story is that we succeeded and we have a wonderful family with siblings close and caring. But at the beginning it was difficult. The children were saddled with a new parent and were still grieving about the death of a parent. We made it a point to have mention of the deceased parents a normal event, which has continued to this day. We even had photos of our first marriages on our family picture wall. We both loved our first spouses and we wanted our children to know and realize that. However, we also wanted them to realize that life must go on and Moe and I were both very grateful that we had a second chance to love and admire someone. I felt especially lucky since it takes a special man to be comfortable with a professionally successful woman and not to feel threatened by her. Moe has been so successful and outstanding in his career that he can be as proud of my success as I am of his.

At the beginning it was not easy. We would joke with tears in our eyes, as we would figure the combinations, as the children would form ranks. There was also the additional fifth person in the combination since Lucy had continued to work with us after we married. She had problems with another woman in the house. This, too, worked out and we have remained friends with Lucy to this day. Moe gave her away when she married Gene Herring, and we watched with pleasure her children growing up into successful adults. We attended weddings of her children as she attended those of ours. We flew up to her youngest son Steven's recital as he graduated from Julliard.

We continued to look for a house without success. Many homes with five bedrooms had one of them in the basement and we did not want that since we did not want any child to feel that he or she was being put in the basement. Finally, I checked with the builder of my house and learned that he was building some homes in Luxmanor, a Bethesda community near Rockville off Old Georgetown Road. We could afford it if we were careful. It would be finished over the summer while we were planning to go to the laboratory in Mt. Desert, Maine. That way we could move in on our return and the children could start in their new schools at the beginning of the term. While we were sorry to make the children change schools, it seemed the only solution.

One night at dinner Moe asked if I still had my strong

objections to going to Germany. I told him that I would only go under extraordinary circumstances. He told me that he had been invited to a meeting near Munich with all expenses paid for both of us. Since at this point we were both somewhat overwhelmed about trying to cope with melding our families, I jumped at the opportunity and told him that this was certainly an extraordinary circumstance. Moe's mother volunteered to stay with the children and did a good job of it although she had her bag packed and was ready to walk out of the door the minute we returned. Moe and I had a marvelous trip. Getting away, we were able to reestablish our close love for each other. We realized that to stay sane the two of us would have to get away every so often by ourselves and we continued to do so. Since Moe had never been to Europe we started in London and also had a few days in Paris. We had met Father Martin McCarthy, a Jesuit priest astronomer at Castel Gandolfo, when he was at Georgetown University. He was one of Vera's instructors. He became a friend of hers and also of all our family. We told him we were visiting Rome and on our arrival at our hotel we were treated as very important people since there was a large envelope from the Vatican waiting for us. Martin had arranged for us to visit many special places at the Vatican and also to attend Wednesday mass. He had told them we were newlyweds (but, not that we were Jewish) and on our arrival for it Moe had to go to a very special building (no women allowed) to get our passes. We were given a medal for Moe (later we learned for fertility) and I was given a mother of pearl cross so we could have the pope bless them during the mass. We also bought a number of crucifixes to be blessed and given to Catholic friends. We were seated up front along with a number of young couples and at a point in the service, the Pope asked the newlyweds to stand to be blessed. We stood with the others and it was quite moving. We had dinner each evening with Martin. One night Moe asked him to order the wine and he ordered a wine we would not find in the United States. We all laughed when the bottle arrived with a big label that said it was bottled especially for Macy's in New York. We spent one day with him at Castel Gandolfo and since the Pope was not in residence we were able to tour the special garden used by the Pope and see the telescope there. We then went by bus with Martin on his Vespa to a nearby town where the owner of a small restaurant to whom Martin had been quite helpful when his wife had died, made a special meal for us.

We only spent the actual meeting time in Germany. I met some wonderful colleagues of Moe's from all over the world, including Germany. I realized what I knew in theory—you cannot condemn an entire population and must meet people as individuals. Of course, many Germans that I met had not been born or were only children during the Hitler years since it was now many years after the Holocaust. Some we met felt quite guilty about what had happened and were able to discuss it. We were close to Dachau. We, together with Frank Epstein and Izzy Adelman, Jewish doctors, also from the United States, felt that we could not be there without visiting it. Therefore, one afternoon, we hired a taxi to visit the concentration camp. It was quite an emotional experience. Seeing the actual camp and the gas chambers is something I will never forget. The camp had been made into a historical area. There was even a German standing on a platform with a microphone shouting "never again." So, we learned that guilt was shared by many Germans. The experience was something never to be forgotten.

Until the children outgrew it, we had wonderful summer times at the Mt. Desert Island Biological Laboratory. We would overload our station wagon with Moe's scientific equipment and our gear and drive to Newton Center to overnight with Moe's parents. We would then drive on to Maine after adding to our load food from the Newton Center Market. Moe's father, Charlie, who was the owner, was always generous enough to have it charged to him. Since we had one of the largest families we were given Burns cabin to use. It had a bedroom on the first floor and loft bedrooms on both sides of the cabin. One had stairs to it and the other had a pull-down ladder used to climb up to the loft. The boys used that one. There was only one bathroom so the boys would often use the woods. The children were surprised that there was only one bathroom since ours in Bethesda had three and the house we were building had 4 ½. We thought this was a good experience for them to realize that that is not true for everybody. On arrival at the cabin Moe would line the children up and place marks on the wall for their heights. That way we could visualize how much each one had grown during the year. Years later when Moe and I visited the lab, I drove to the cabin and was invited in by the present occupants. The marks were still there and I was excited to see them. The residents were delighted to learn the history of the marks and said that they had continued the practice, marking the height of each of their children each summer when they arrived at the lab. One day Moe had discovered the entire cabin had only one circuit and one fuse. He rewired it. Despite its limited space and kitchen, I was able to make dinner one time for 35. The children were helpful in quickly setting up tables for everyone after we had had appetizers. It worked quite well.

Our dinner menus became repetitive. One night we had steamed clams (after Moe had put them into the aquarium at the lab to free them of sand). The next night we had lump crab that I purchased from a widow of a lobsterman, who lived a few miles away and had cleaned them. Fishermen gave her the crabs caught in their nets and she would pick the meat out and sell it. The third night we had Maine chicken. The fourth we had lobster. The fisherman who caught the fish for lab experiments was a lobsterman. He kept a trap at the end of the pier. Moe would get down on his belly and reach into the trap and pull out the lobsters. He would weight them on the lab scale and convert the kilos into pounds. We would place the money ($1.00 per pound) in an envelope and leave it in the mail cubicle for the fisherman. We would then get a pail of seawater and cook the lobsters in it at our cabin. There is nothing like freshly caught lobster and it has spoiled my taste for restaurant lobster ever since—though I admit I still do eat and enjoy it.

I had never been camping, but Moe was a camper. My first experience was at a beautiful lake in Maine near Mt. Katahdin. Moe helped us set up camp and then left me alone with the girls while he went off for the night with the boys to an island in the middle of the lake for overnight. I managed. We spent a number of more weekends camping. I fell in love with camping and continued to enjoy it for many years. In later years most of our camping was in the wilderness rather than at places where you could drive up and unload your gear. My friends could not believe that I enjoyed camping since they knew me as the girl who wanted the best room in the best hotel wherever we went. We did not socialize that much with others at the lab. They had daily cocktail parties that really did not interest us. We preferred to go canoeing and fishing with the children.

At the end of our 1967 stay in Maine I called to make certain that our new house was ready for occupancy and was assured it was. Of course, when we returned to Bethesda, it was not ready so we essentially camped in it for several days as it as was completed. We had lots of furniture (from two households) but no furniture for the 23-foot living room, so that remained empty. Larry's bar mitzvah was shortly after we returned from Maine. We had not had a reception for friends when we married since we did not want presents, so we decided to have the party for Larry's bar mitzvah as a way for friends to get to meet our new spouses. It was at Succoth since Larry wanted it at the same time Max had had his bar mitzvah in Germany. It worked out fine. Rabbi Lipman dedicated the house and put up the mezuzah.

When we could afford it, we started to furnish our living room. That is how we met Victor Shargai who has remained a close friend and our decorator for nearly 50 years. Through Victor we also became quite friendly with his partner, John Aniello. We mourned John's too early death about 10 years ago. We are very happy that Victor and Craig Pascal are now together. They are both wonderful people who we are glad to have as friends.

We had filed documents so that we could cross adopt our new children. Since they were old enough, they had to consent to the adoptions and were suspicious of what this would mean. They finally consented, and we all went to court for the judge to speak with each of them in chambers and get their consents. Since there was no living other parent, this was less complicated than where there is a divorced parent who also has to consent and at times fights it. So we now had a complete family—at least in the eyes of the law. We continued to have problems, however. Many of them were the usual teen-age problems. However, superimposed on these problems were the complications of the new marriage and objections from Moe's first in-laws, who were opposed to his remarrying. They would not have anything to do with us and were determined to keep "their grandchildren" separate. At times we would get phone calls from Moe's mother asking about the children in such a way that it was apparent that a letter had gone to her about the wicked stepmother. We continued to work on the situation. While, if I had to do it over again, there are certain things I would have done differently, I am grateful that today we do have a wonderful family. I constantly kept in mind Aunt Helen's statement that most parents are not perfect but they are trying to do what is best. I dearly loved and was concerned for all my children and am annoyed when asked who were Moe's and who were mine. I quickly respond they are all mine and I really feel and believed that, even when some doubts are expressed. I recognize that our children's' lives were difficult. Today there are counselors and clinical psychologists who are different than they were in the 1950-1960 era. Whether this would have made any difference I do not know. I do know that today we have four wonderful children. I admit at times there are the usual family flare ups, but we put that behind us. We are one family and I am happy and grateful for it.

While in Maine we visited the Old Town canoe factory and bought the last mahogany gunnel large canoe they ever made. We drove around with it mounted on the roof of our station wagon and had many happy adventures with it. Each of the years that we spent at Mt. Desert Moe would take a two-week vacation and we would go off to an interesting spot. One year we went to a campsite near Mt. Katahdin and Moe, Betsy, Larry and Bobby climbed to the top of the mountain. Joan and I stayed below. When they returned, Moe had the boys turn and bend over so we could see that their jeans had worn through from sliding down some of the slopes. On our way to the mountain we had stopped at Kidney Pond and saw a fisherman out in a canoe on the lake. Moe recognized him as a colleague from California. We called to him and this is how I met Donald Marsh. We have remained friends over all these years. Don and his wife, Wendy Clough, are part of our New Year's Gang. The gang is now reduced to just our two couples since the others do not want to travel to Florida for New Year's. More about the gang later.

One summer while in Maine we had a great camping trip to Nova Scotia, crossing on the Blue Nose Ferry from Mt Desert. I remember the fields of ripe wild strawberries that Moe, Larry and I came upon one day while Betsy, Joan and Bobby stayed at our beach campsite. Moe took pictures of Larry and me with the knees of our jeans bright red from kneeling as we picked and ate the wonderful, sweet berries. On our trip home we had car trouble and Moe hoped we would get back without trouble. He was wrong. When we drove off the Blue Nose ferry and got in line for customs the car stalled. We were pushed out of line and the inspecting officer required us to open the spare tire storage bin to make sure we had no contraband. He was sorry he made Moe do this since it meant unloading the entire car of all our camping gear. Once we passed inspection we continued on with four very sleepy children (it was after midnight) and returned to our cabin. The car was repaired the next day. I have many other wonderful memories of our summers at the lab—the fresh popovers and delicious ice cream from the Jordon Pond House that we devoured after climbing Mt. Sergeant and Mt. Penobscot (two mountains with a beautiful lake on the path connecting them), picking wonderful blueberries on Mt. Cadillac and making pancakes and muffins from them, and fishing from the canoe.

One year we took a ten-day canoe camping trip on Lake Allagash. We rented two additional canoes and were driven to a drop off point in the wilderness. As the truck that brought us drove off to pick us up ten days later, Betsy came to us and told us that, speaking for all her siblings, they were going under protest. Today they tell us that this trip was a highlight of their times in Maine and they have no recollection of such an announcement. But we do! We loaded the canoes and set off. Betsy and Bobby were in the first canoe and as they took off Betsy was excited by the "fountain" spouting up from the center of their canoe. Moe yelled to them to return to shore since they were sinking. He determined that one of the screws that fastened the ribs at the bottom of the canoe was missing. We were alone miles from nowhere with no one returning for ten days. He filled the hole with a screw from near the top of the canoe and placed the hole that was left with a shard of pine and pine tar. It worked during our entire trip. There were campsites along the lake and we spent each night at a different site as we circumnavigated the lake. We ate freeze-dried food for the entire trip and Moe tried, without success, to catch fish to supplement our meals. On the last day, as we paddled down the middle of the lake, Moe continued trolling from the rear of the canoe. He hooked a huge lake trout and stood up in the loaded canoe to play the fish. With me screaming he should sit down, Moe told me to net the fish. Luckily I was able to do so. We camped our final night on an island across from our pick up spot. We dined on fresh trout and ripe blueberries we picked in a field on the island. It was a feast we savored after ten days of freeze dried food.

Our last summer at Mt. Desert we rented a house on

Long Pond since Moe decided not to deal with transporting all his equipment up to the lab. Moe commuted to and from NIH to Bangor for two-week stints. Each morning I had a fresh bass for breakfast. When Moe was not there, Larry, who had become quite a good angler, caught one for me. This was our last summer at Mt. Desert. We made one more trip years later to a meeting there. Carl Gottschalk, a close friend from University of North Carolina, met Susan Fellner at that meeting. Carl's wife had died a few years earlier and he and I spent long walks as I reassured him that life would go on. He and Susan married several years later and we spent many happy times with them until Carl tragically died. Susan, also a nephrologist, still remains a close friend.

After that summer in Maine we began to explore various wilderness areas in the West. We would be packed into a wilderness by horse and left for a designated time. The packer would then return and we would ride out. We generally would stay at a place for a week or longer. We eventually fell in love with the Sawtooth Wilderness where Jeff and Debby Bitten had Mystic Saddle Ranch. They packed us into the Sawtooth for fourteen summers. We would stay anywhere from three days to three weeks depending on the time available. Family and friends often went with us. Moe prepared all the food—freeze dried of course—and fresh food was the trout Moe caught in the beautiful lakes there. The ride in included Sand Pass over a narrow path with huge drops on either side. It took me about ten years to be able to open my eye as we went over the pass so that I could enjoy the beautiful vistas around us. Until then I would scream hysterically when Moe wanted to stop to take a picture of the view.

I was hesitant to invest in stock since I never knew when a litigant might be a parent or subsidiary of a company. Therefore, until the federal tax laws changed, we invested in condos that we would lease back to the company to rent for us. This was fun because it gave us an opportunity to visit the areas to inspect our investments and we could stay for two weeks without many tax consequences. We purchased condos in Captiva Island, Florida, and spent time there with our parents and family since we did not like Miami, where Moe's parents had retired, or Lake Wales where my parents had retired. Little did we know that we would end up living in Miami someday, although it is much different now than it was then. Also, we are older! We also had three different condos sequentially in Sun Valley, Idaho. This was close to the Sawtooth and we stored all our camping gear at Sun Valley once we made the Sawtooth our annual wilderness location. In 1986, Richard Klatt built our beautiful home on

Hebgen Lake outside of West Yellowstone, Montana. We have spent many happy hours there with family and friends or by ourselves. Richard and Jackie became and remain great friends. We sold the Sun Valley condo since we no longer used it and there were no tax advantages any more. We sold the Captiva condo and time-share when our parents no longer were able to visit us there.

We also travelled to many wonderful locations where Moe was invited to speak or where we attended international meetings. I learned how much more exciting it is to visit foreign lands as guests rather than as tourists. I wish I had kept a diary of all the places we visited. We had marvelous trips to Japan where we were housed in ryokans by our hosts, trips to Israel, Switzerland, France, China, Belgium, Denmark, Finland, Sweden, Hungary (behind the iron curtain), Germany, Czechoslovakia, and Botswana to mention just a few. In 1975, I had to turn down an all-expense-paid trip to Lebanon with Moe since I was presiding over a major six-month trial so could not accompany him. I also had trials in Thailand with a stopover in Hong Kong (Moe joined me on this trip) and in Italy, Germany, Japan and Okinawa. So we got to see a lot of the world.

On our trips to the wilderness, I several times purchased a backpacking spinning fishing rod. Somehow it always got lost early on the trip. I finally got the hint and learned to fly fish—Moe's specialty. While I never became as expert as he, I became a pretty good angler and fell in love with it. So, in addition to our business trips, we made winter trips to the southern hemisphere to fly fish. We went to New Zealand fourteen times and then made a number of trips to Chile and Argentina. While we saw few of the tourist attractions in these countries, we got to know the fishing areas much better. Moe often combined these trips with lectures or visits to former fellows so; again, we saw these places not as tourists but as guests.

Back home in Bethesda, we learned to our dismay that the public schools near us did not live up to the standard of many Montgomery county schools. Larry asked to transfer from Woodward High School to Walter Johnson but we turned him down since that school had such a bad drug reputation. It might have been a bad decision but we were trying to do our best. Since both Moe and I had been public school graduates, we felt that public schools were the way to go. This might have been a bad decision since it was a different time but we participated in the PTA and thought all was okay. When Joan asked to transfer to Walt Whitman High School, a much more difficult school, we realized that things were really bad. Betsy and Larry were quite dissatisfied with Woodward and we realized that they would probably never even graduate if we did not make a change. We investigated various possibilities and based on recommendations from consultants and doctors, Betsy and Larry each went to boarding school for the senior year at high school. Betsy went to Sandy Springs Friends School and Larry to one in the Berkshires in Massachusetts that had been highly recommended. It was hard to have them away from home but we were trying to do our best. When Bobby finished elementary school we enrolled him in Georgetown Day School and he did middle and high school there.

1972-2016

In 1972, Paul discussed my future plans and, learning that I liked the judicial side of the law, contacted Richard Sollibakke, Chairman of the Armed Services Board of Contract Appeals (ASBCA). This was by far the largest and best board, and appointments were on merit, not political pull. Dick knew me as Paul's assistant but nothing else about my professional career. I was invited for an interview and offered an appointment as a judge at the board. This required approval by the Under Secretaries of Defense, Army, Navy and Air Force but rarely was refused. There were no women on the board of 38 judges and they were looking for a qualified woman to appoint and offered me the next vacancy. I became a member late in 1972. The board was divided into 3 divisions. Dan Arons was my division head until he became vice-chairman of the board. He became a good friend and I mourned his death from melanoma when he was much too young. He was a brilliant jurist and a wonderful opinion writer. I learned a great deal from him.

I enjoyed being a judge. The work was difficult and challenging. Since I was the first woman appointed to our board, many attorneys appearing before me were very suspicious of my ability to understand their issues. Because of my experience with builders, I could understand construction questions and read blue prints more easily than many of my male colleagues. I have many stories of experiences that I had being the only woman on the board. I laughed about most of them and am putting some of the more interesting or funny ones here. I had many difficult cases and created law in the area of my specialty. I am told that my reputation was that I was tough but fair and so I feel I earned my keep. Of course, there were some who lost their cases who felt I made the wrong decision. But they had the opportunity to appeal in most cases.

TALES OF EXPERIENCES AS A WOMAN JUDGE

I was the first and only woman judge at the ASBCA for eight years following my appointment in 1972. In those days the world of defense contracting was almost entirely male both among the suppliers and the government personnel. This led to a number of amusing incidents during those early years until I established my reputation of knowing what I was doing. There were very few woman judges at that time and this was an additional problem. Every stage of government defense contracting from designing the requirements to establishing the budget to making the procurement, to inspecting and accepting the product, and all the stages in between were done by the mostly male military and, especially in the large procurements for ships, weapons and other defense items, it was an all-male world. I was, at various times, taken for a court reporter, a secretary or clerk. Many procurements involved blue prints and attorneys would go to great lengths to make certain I could read them. They never challenged my male colleagues who could not do so. I had no problem with blueprints since my law practice had included many builders and blueprints were second nature for me.

One of the most outstanding experiences, which I still tease the private counsel about even today, involved a site visit as I prepared to try a nuclear submarine dispute in 1975. Site visits are always an issue since rarely can a court reporter be present and there is a constant concern that something will be said about the dispute. No summary is ever as good as an actual view. I had agreed to lunch with the parties if both sides were represented. I was seated across from the Navy Captain and the president of the shipyard at a long table of about 30-40 diners (all male, of course). The president of the shipyard told me his views on the role of women during the course of our conversations, namely that they should all be home tending house and raising children. I led him on for about 20 minutes as he elaborated on his theories to the woman (me) who would decide what at that time was the largest claim we had ever had ($120,000,000 in 1975). I had a ball, much to the discomfort of the attorneys for the shipyard. They had warned him not to discuss the case or to voice his thought that it was "stupid" that I had insisted I would only dine with them if I could pay for my own lunch, but it had never occurred to them to warn him not to discuss his view of the proper role of women!

We borrowed courtrooms in various cities, since we literally rode circuit. One time, while in San Francisco, it became apparent that a man and I were both looking for the same courtroom. He asked if I was the court reporter and was taken aback when I told him that I was the judge. He should have known this since he was the Chief Trial Attorney for the Navy. He got his comeuppance later that day. Moe was in the courtroom watching the proceedings since he had time before speaking at the University of California Medical School. During a recess when I did not leave the bench, he asked someone to take a note to me since he had to leave. The person he asked was the Chief Trial Attorney who, startled, did as asked and brought the note to me—a job generally left to his underlings.

During a much too long trial, a master sergeant on the stand testified that it took no longer to polish stainless steel kitchen equipment until it had no streaks than to wipe down white enamel equipment. I called counsel to my chambers and told them that they had the wrong judge because I had cleaned too many kitchens to believe such nonsense and ordered them to discuss settlement. They did and settled the case.

There were many other instances where counsel made it clear that they thought I could not understand the complexities of the issues. I would make it clear that I did understand the subject matter and issues by asking questions of the witness. Over the years it became clear to the trial community that I knew what I was doing, so such doubts were resolved. Today this is no longer an issue for women who are appointed. However, it does not prevent attorneys even today of criticizing losing a case because a woman has decided it!

Over the years I received many awards for my work so I guess that indicates success. I will not list them here but will attach an appendix listing them. I will mention the

Margaret Brent Award given by the Commission on Women of the American Bar Association. It was awarded at a luncheon of several thousand. I am grateful to Pat Wittie and Allan Joseph and other members of the section for their hard work in sponsoring me. My mentors, Marshall Doke, David Hirsch and Allan Joseph were instrumental in my becoming active in the Public Contract Law Section and I served as its first woman chair in 1985. In turn, I am proud to have mentored many persons in the section and am still friendly with them. John Pachter and Mary Ellen Coster Williams have gone on to activity at the House of Delegates. Pat Wittie and Carol Park-Conroy have become very close friends.

I made many friends in the Section and they honored me for my efforts by establishing the Ruth Cooper Burg luncheon held every year at the annual ABA meeting. The luncheon was the development of what we had called the gang of four. At one time only four women attended the Public Contract Law Section meetings at the annual American Bar Association meeting—Patricia (Pat) Szeervo, Carol Lister (General Counsel of the Air Force), Mary Ann Gileece and myself. We would lunch together at the meeting and, as more women attended the meeting, it grew into an informal luncheon for those present. When Mary Ellen Coster Williams chaired the section a number of years later, many of the attendees were women. She suggested and received permission from the section to establish an annual luncheon for men and women celebrating the women in public contracting. It is now the opening event for our section at the annual meeting and I am quite honored to have it named after me.

At one of our anniversaries of the section's existence, the "pioneers" were honored and our photos were shown on a huge screen. The nine men submitted very formal photos in dark jackets and ties. I submitted one in my waders kneeling in a beautiful New Zealand stream holding a five-pound trout I had just landed. My photo was the big hit. On my 85th birthday, there was a surprise birthday party at one of our meetings. I was actually surprised and quite touched by the affection that many members showed to me. I have a beautiful jewelry box that I treasure, presented to me there. At the section luncheon the day before I received the Margaret Brent award, Allan Joseph and Marshall Doke roasted me. They are two wonderful friends I had made in our section. They were such close friends that I had to recuse myself from any of their cases much to my regret, since I consider them two of the best attorneys I ever had appear before me.

I was considered for several other judicial appointments but never had the political backing needed for such appointments during the time that the Democrats were in power and I was young enough to be considered. In retrospect, I do not think I would have enjoyed appellate work as much as trial work. I did head the list for appointment to what is now the Court of Federal Claims but was never appointed. That was an appointment by the Court of Claims judges at the time although it later became a nomination by the President and confirmation by the Senate. I am told that when the judges were making the appointment one of the more influential judges was to have said that while he had any say "that Jew girl will never be appointed." I feel they lost more than I did, since I was experienced in three of the areas in which they heard cases—pubic contract law, tax law and patent law. That is rarely the case with their appointees.

I became a division head at the board and enjoyed my 22 years on the bench there. It entailed a lot of travel both in the United States and overseas since the US has contracts all over the world. At times it was a lonesome travel unless I knew someone not involved in any of the cases I was trying, but often there was so much preparation required I ate in my hotel room or on a military base where I was staying. I travelled with the rank of General so I would be given good quarters on a base if there was one nearby.

For several years after my appointment, my commute to the board was really quite onerous. I had to drive the Virginia part of the Beltway before it was widened and I would often be caught in horrible traffic jams. One Saturday Moe and I were lunching in Georgetown and, after some wine, talked about how lovely it would be to live there and be able to walk out to enjoy such meals. I came up with a number of reasons why it would not work but Moe had an explanation for each of them. As a result, I began to look for a home in Georgetown. We needed a house that was within our price range and that was large enough to accommodate the children when they came home from school or living away. It took a while, but I received a call about a house that was going on the market over Columbus Day. We were going to be away for that weekend but on our return, we immediately looked at it. We signed a contract for 3106 Que Street on the sidewalk as we first walked out of it.

The house was in terrible shape and had to be gutted completely. It took six months to complete the renovations, and, when we moved in there was still work to be done. I still remember Victor Shargai busily sweeping out the hallway as the moving truck arrived. Victor did a wonderful job renovating. At Moe's father's suggestion we replaced all the old iron plumbing so we would not have to tear out walls later. We had a large garden, 120 feet long, and had a wonderful time landscaping it. The basement had a maid's bedroom and bath that were horrible and looked like slave quarters. It was shocking to me that the previous owner had her maid live there while she lived alone in the four bedrooms upstairs. We renovated the basement room into a little office and tore out the bath and never replaced it. The front of the full basement was large enough for Moe's tools and it was here that he finished his grandfather clock, copied from the English antique original at the metropolitan Museum. He had already made an oak breakfast table and benches with Gothic carvings and a Chinese table in his workshop in Luxmanor. We still treasure all these pieces today. The house had three bedrooms and two baths on the second floor and a bedroom and bath in the front part of the attic. We moved one bed and mattress from each of the children's rooms so there was one room for the girls and one for the boys. We wanted them to have a familiar bed and dresser when they came to stay with us. In later years we raised the roof on the back part of the attic and cantilevered a greenhouse off the third floor there. That took quite an engineering job. I loved the house and if the steps had not been so steep, making it impossible for me with my bad knees to navigate them, we would be living there today.

While we were still living in Luxmanor, our nephew David Ruben married and had to give up his dog, Huxley, because his wife was allergic to dogs. We gave in to our children's pressuring us for a dog and agreed that Huxley could come live with us if he stayed in a structure in the garden. That condition evaporated very quickly and Huxley became a major part of our family. He was a wonderful dog. He was very intelligent, understood many words and moved with us to Georgetown. He looked like a black bear and, when we would walk him in Georgetown, rowdy teenagers would immediately quiet down after one bark from him. He loved ice cream and would catch a cone thrown up in air as it was on its way down. He was great at begging for ice cream in front of Hagen Das. We replaced him when he died with a wonderful blond Labrador, Stuart, whom we all came to love. Stuart was marvelous with children and when our oldest granddaughter, Maureen, learned to crawl she would crawl right over him without his moving a muscle. When he became too lame to walk, Larry would carry him outside when needed. We miss Huxley and Stuart, but because of our frequent travel, we did not get another dog.

Lucy Herring took time off to have her children. One

day we received a call from a woman who wanted a reference to hire Lucy. Moe had not become hearing impaired as he is today and was the one who took the call. When he heard her question he told her that if Lucy was looking for work she was going to work for us. When she persisted in knowing if we would give Lucy a reference, he repeated what he had told her and, upon hanging up, immediately called Lucy. She returned to work with us the next day.

Friday was our family night at home. The children were expected to be there and were welcome to bring friends. When we moved to Georgetown they frequently came for Friday dinner and we were thrilled to have them do so. We used the good china and silver and celebrated the Sabbath. Lucy was an excellent cook and she had learned to make wonderful matzah ball soup and other goodies. The first Friday after Lucy returned, her husband, Gene, arrived to pick her up after dinner with their children all dressed up. We were thrilled to see them. I still remember her oldest son, Greg, standing at the living room and staring at the 23 feet of bookcases filled with books from floor to ceiling. He said he had never seen so many books in a house before. Today, most of our books are on our computers and the bookcases are long gone. When we moved from Georgetown, we gave thousands of books to Lucy's church. Many went to Africa including a set of encyclopedias Moe had purchased with his Bar Mitzvah money. Lucy said they were better than what existed in some towns.

I met Moe's friend, Charles Young, an oncologist at Sloan Kettering, the first summer we spent together at Mt. Desert. Our families became great friends and we visited them in their apartment in New York and enjoyed performances at the Metropolitan Opera together with them. We even had a surprise reunion with Charlie one time in Paris when we were at a meeting of the International Society of Nephrology. Charlie was there at another professional event. Somehow he learned of our presence and tracked us down It was fun and a surprise to lunch together in Paris. Charlie and his wife, Helene, began spending New Years with us in Washington. Shortly thereafter we were joined by Don Marsh, then Chairman of Physiology at the University of California and later Dean of Brown Medical School, and his wife, Wendy Clough, also a physician, my sister, Vera and her husband, Bob Rubin, and Ann Garfinkle, an attorney in DC and her husband Joseph Brent, an historian. That became our New Year's Gang that assembled for many wonderful years. Most years we celebrated in Washington but some years we met in New York City. There was one memorable year when a ten-inch snowfall in New York did not deter us. Because prices were exorbitant in New York for the millennium, we celebrated New Years in New York in October. Daniel's Restaurant even printed a menu with that title for our special dinner there. Our number decreased when Bob Rubin died and became even smaller when Moe and I started wintering in Miami. Now only Don and Wendy join us. We still have a great time but we reminisce about the wonderful years our gang celebrated together and hope we may do so again in the future.

I retired from the ASBCA in 1995. In those days a large dinner was given for someone retiring from the board. Today it has become quite simple with a small luncheon at the board itself. My retirement was at a dinner at Fort Meyer and there were several hundred people present. I was quite flattered by the persons who made the effort to attend and the speeches that were made. My whole family was present. My older granddaughter, Maureen, had a great time with Loren Smith, Chief Judge of the Court of Federal Claims, an amateur magician, who did some magic tricks for her. At a meeting of the Public Contract Law Section, I was honored at a reception. I was given one of our section's pins surrounded by diamonds (I am the only person who has one like this) and a beautifully bound book with an index and abstracts of many of my decisions that was prepared by Marshall Doke, one of the friends I had made through our section. There was a series of blank pages in the back upon which many of our members wrote messages. I was extremely touched by what they had to say and hold the book as one of my favorite treasures.

Our daughters are both happily married. Betsy married Michael Kelley in 1981. They have two lovely daughters, Maureen and Louise. After her husband, Chris Borton's, tragic death at the age of 33, Joan became close to his business partner and friend, Dolf Starreveld and they married in November 1999. They have a wonderful son, Max, whose bar mitzvah we celebrated last year. Unfortunately, Larry's marriages were not as successful. Bob owns a home outside of Boston and keeps busy with his coin business.

After my retirement, I acted as an arbitrator or mediator and enjoyed it very much. Arbitration was quite similar to a trial except there were generally three people acting together rather than just a single judge presiding. I liked mediation more since it is often over more quickly and the parties, not the judge or arbitrator, made the decision. The challenge was to help steer the parties to settle the matter. This often meant you ended with two unhappy parties rather than just one where a decision was made for them, but, after the initial disappointment, they generally are happy to have the dispute behind them. I did no advertising or marketing and my cases were based on my reputation. I had sufficient cases to keep me as busy as I wanted with time for family, friends and travelling with Moe. I was paid far better than I was as a judge, since judges are notoriously underpaid. I often had first year associates making far more than I did. Both Moe and I loved what we were doing and were not sorry that we had chosen the lowest paid areas of our professions. I used some of the funds I earned for family travel. We had trips to the Galapagos, Costa Rica and Tanzania that were memorable.

In addition Moe and I continued our winter trips to the southern hemisphere to fish. We also managed trips to Alaska for wonderful fishing there. Once Moe became a Scientist Emeritus at NIH in 2014, we were able to spend our entire summer at our home in Montana. It was great to be able to avoid the commuting (two weeks in Montana, two at NIH) that we had done for many years. I still take time for attending the annual ABA meetings held in late July or early August and now Moe can come with me. We also had a wonderful trip to China, when Moe was invited to speak there, and marvelous trips by the two of us to India and Morocco.

We celebrated landmark events by trips with our children and grandchildren to the Galapagos, Costa Rica and Tanzania. We also had eventful trips with our grandchildren. The first was a Harvard family trip that I took with our granddaughters, Maureen and Louise when they were 8 and 4 years old. Since they roomed with other children, I invited our daughters, Betsy and Joan, to share my room. We cruised the Mediterranean from Genoa to Istanbul and back to Venice with memorable stops along the way. Several years later, we visited Paris with all the Kelleys since Maureen wanted to see the Eifel Tower and knew she had a good customer in me. When the girls were older we had a great trip to London and Bath and places in between with just Maureen and Louise. We had a wonderful trip to Israel with our daughter, Joan, her husband, Dolf, and their son, Max, so that three generations could visit Israel together.

Moe's professional travel is much reduced these days. My private work as a neutral has also fallen off. Younger attorneys know my name, not me, so are interested in younger neutrals. In 2014 we were headed to Chile for Moe to meet with former fellows, to speak in Santiago and to fish at a favorite lodge. We decided to spend a few weeks in Miami on our way since we no longer enjoy the cold. .While in Miami, I developed pneumonia and instead of Chile, spent the time at Mt. Sinai Hospital. While recuperating we enjoyed the cultural activates of Miami and Miami South Beach and their outstanding restaurants, so we bought a condo here. We now spend our winters in Miami Beach, our summers in Montana and the spring and fall in Washington, DC. We remain in DC for the Maurice Burg annual lecture that NIH established in his honor and then fly to Miami. Those of our children willing to do so join us in Florida for Thanksgiving. While we miss the annual Thanksgiving reunion at our daughter Betsy's, the warm weather wins out. Our long trips to foreign shores are probably a thing of the past but we cannot complain. We have seen and experienced a lot and are grateful for it.

As I approach my 90th birthday and Moe his 85th, we celebrate our 48th anniversary as husband and wife. They have been a marvelous 48 years. There have been sad events along the way, but being able to rebound from them is what life is all about. I have had two good marriages. Moe's and my love has matured and ripened over the years. We have a wonderful family, four great children, two great sons-in-law and three wonderful grandchildren. Moe and I are grateful for having a "second chance." We love each other deeply and respect each other's achievements. While I would probably do some things differently, I have tried to do my best. My life has been rich and rewarding and I hope the years remaining to me bring additional good events. I have been called a pioneer in my profession. I am proud of the achievements of the many young women (and men, too) whom I have mentored along the way. To me, that is my most outstanding professional achievement.

I have spent most of these pages on my earlier years since this has been written primarily at the request of and as information for our children. They have been old enough to remember the more recent years and, as I said earlier, it is for them, not me, to record their lives and development. As they read this, maybe they can learn a little more of what and whom I am and what has made me tick. However, I would be remiss if I did not mention how much Moe has always been there over the years. His encouragement when times seemed rough, his taking charge when travel took me away from home and his love and loyalty have helped make it all possible. He did this while remaining outstanding in his own profession. I will not name all his awards and achievements. I hope he will do so since they have been outstanding. I will mention the thrills I have experienced in being with him when he received them. I name some of them: seeing him walk across the stage to sign the great book as he was inducted into the National Academy of Sciences and being at the annual lectureship established in his honor at the National Institutes of Health. I am very proud of him. My husband and my family have been the most important things in my life. They have always come first in any decisions I have made. My career has always come behind and I have no regrets in that regard.

All told it has been an exciting and wonderful ride.

PHOTOS

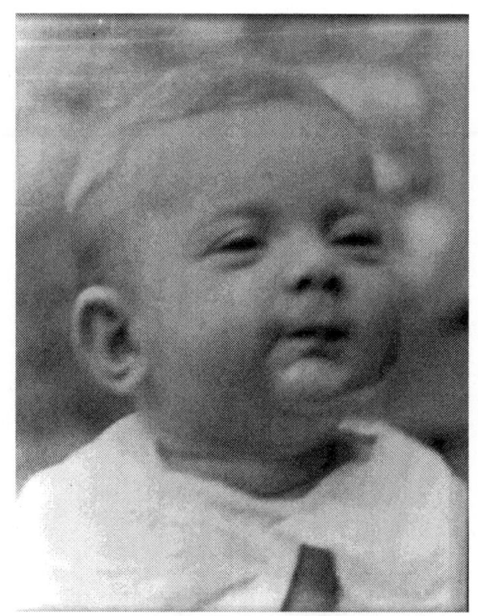

Ruth at 6 months

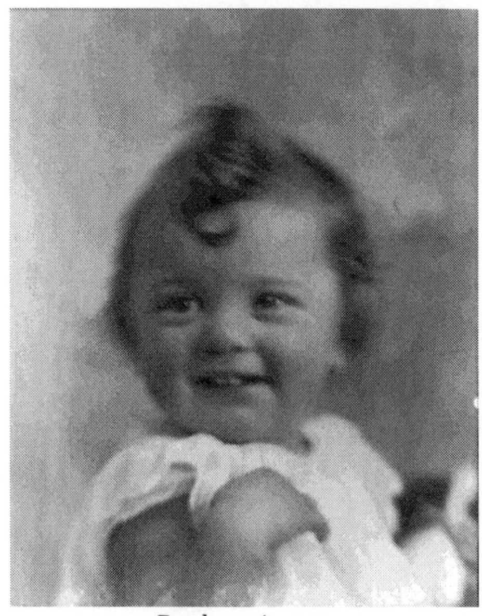

Ruth at 1 year

Ruth (4) and Vera (2) at Sydney Street

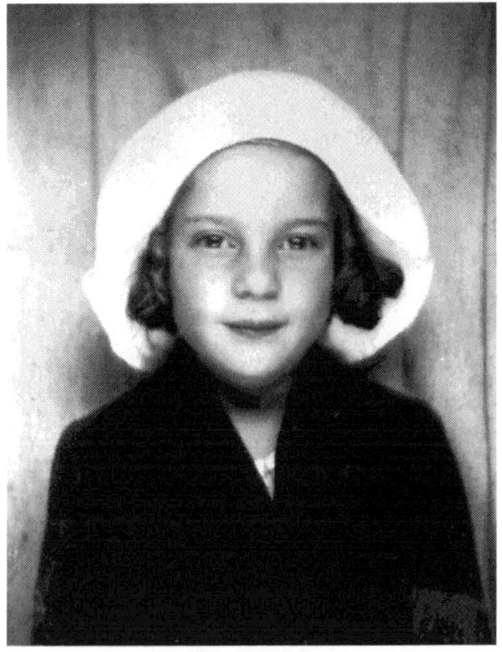
Ruth at 6

Parents Rose and Pete, Vera and Ruth 1945

Max and Ruth, Wedding 1946

George Washington Law Review Editors

Receiving John Bell Larner Medal from GW President Lloyd Marvin for graduating first in Class 1950

Law School Graduation 1950

Max, Larry, Ruth, Joan 1957

Larry, Ruth, Max, Joan 1963

Moe and Ruth Wedding 1967

Joan, Ruth, Bob, Larry, Moe, Betsy
Wedding 1967

Irene's Cabin with Family and Friends 1970

China 1980

Judge Burg

Past Chairs Public Contract Law Section 20th Anniversary, 1990

Allan Joseph, Marshall Doke
Reception Honoring Ruth, 1995

Receiving Distinguished Alumna Award
Fro President Trachtenberg 2001

Fishing in New Zealand 1995

House in Montana

Galapagos 2001

Assada in Chile 2002

Stonehenge with our granddaughters, Maureen and Louise Kelley, 2006

Family in Costa Rica, 2006

Family in Tanzania, 2008

Lunch on Stream Fishing in Argentina, 2009

Brunch at our DC Condo, 2004

New Year Gang, 2007
Helene & Charlie Young,
Ann Garfinkle & Joe Brent,
Vera & Bob Rutin, Ruth,
Don & Wendy Marsh, M

At the Margaret Brent Award, 2008

Family and Friends in the Green Room
Margaret Brent Award 2008

Ruth with Margaret Brent Award 2008

Past Women Chairs of PCL, Karen Hastie Williams, Mary Ellen Coster Williams, Marcia Maden, Pat Meager with Section Director Marilyn Neforas

India, 2011

Argentina with guide Carlos 2012

China 2013

Morocco 2013

Max Starreveld Bar Mitzvah, 2014
Moe, Ruth, Joan, Max & Dolf Starreveld, Bob and Larry

Formal Family Portrait

Awards and Honors

Margaret Brent Women of Achievement Award presented by the American Bar Association Commission on Women in the Profession, August 2008

George Washington University Distinguished Alumna Award May 18-19, 2002

Beatrice Rosenberg Award for Public Service from the District of Columbia Bar Association, March 3, 2000

Fulbright Award for Public Service from George Washington University Law Alumni awarded September 22, 2000

Order of the COIF

John Bell Larner Award—Medal awarded to the George Washington University Law School graduate ranking first in class.

Taxation Editor, George Washington University Law Review

George Washington University Law School, scholarship awardee for second and third years of Law School.

George Washington University scholarship awardee for 4 years undergraduate education.

Valedictorian Calvin Coolidge High School, Washington, D. C., 1943

Bausch & Lomb Medal given to high school graduate most outstanding in science

Ruth C. Burg Luncheon for Women in Public Contract Law (Annual luncheon by the American Bar Association Public Contract Law Section at the annual meeting)

American Bar Assn. Public Contract Law Fellows Spirit of Leadership award, August 2006

"Star of the Bar," Women's Bar Association of the District of Columbia, October 2004

"Star of the Bar," Women's Bar Association of the District of Columbia, October 2008

ABA Commission on Women in the Profession

Women Trailblazers in the Law

ORAL HISTORY

of

RUTH BURG

Interviewer: Estelle Rogers

Dates of Interviews:

October 15, 2005
November 5, 2005
December 17, 2005

INTERVIEW WITH RUTH BURG
BY ESTELLE ROGERS
OCTOBER 15, 2005

Ms. Rogers: First, I would like to start with your early background, and if you'll tell me about where you grew up, what your parents were like, where they came from, and siblings.

Ms. Burg: All right, we'll start with my parents. My father came from Vilna [Vilnius, Lithuania] at age 8, settled in Gloversville, New York with his parents, because my grandfather was in the glove business in Vilna; They left there in about 1914 and moved to Philadelphia where my grandfather opened a glove and corset shop at 52nd and Walnut which in those days was a very lovely neighborhood. I wouldn't vouch for it today. My father went to the University of Pennsylvania and graduated as an electrical engineer.

Ms. Rogers: What year?

Ms. Burg: 1920. He had really wanted to major in mathematics but was told that a Jewish boy couldn't get a job in mathematics so he went into electrical engineering. My mother was born in Philadelphia. My father was born in 1897. My mother was born in Philadelphia in 1900. Her parents had both come from Russia, independently, and met and married in Philadelphia. My grandfather was a tailor and as I grew up my grandmother used to entertain us with sewing buttons on the clothes. His tailor shop was on the 4th floor of their house. Mother went through high school, which in those days was no mean accomplishment, and became a hat designer. But her major love was music, and she actually studied voice. As a matter of fact, she studied with the same teacher as Marian Anderson and knew Marian Anderson because they were in the same class together in high school; Mother's name was Applebaum, her name was Anderson. They sat next to each other alphabetically, and mother said she used to hear this gorgeous booming voice next to her as they would sing in assembly. They knew each other and actually corresponded for most of their lives until Marian Anderson began shaving off some of her age and wasn't as quite as anxious to recognize that they had grown up together. My parents married in 1924 in Philadelphia. Both sets of parents being Orthodox Jews, it was a Orthodox wedding, Men and women were not separated during the wedding and receptions but it took place in one of the very Orthodox synagogues. They met working for Bell Telephone Company. My father continued working there until I guess about 1929 or 1930. He wasn't terribly happy with it and was bored because things weren't moving as quickly as he would have liked. I was born in 1926, first child, and mother always teased me because I was born the night of the first seder and both families who always had major large seders had insisted that they come to them for first seder and to the other family for the second seder. Mother said I got even with them. She ended up in the hospital, I was born and my grandmothers, instead of getting ready for Passover, had to rush to the hospital to see me. My uncle always teased me that I made him break Pesach: - he was so excited, he had an ice cream soda. My sister was born in 1928 and we were the only two children. I think, but for the Depression, there might have been more, but that was hard enough.

Ms. Rogers: Tell me a little bit more about your mother. What was she doing at Bell Telephone?

Ms. Burg: She was a secretary. She also participated-- Bell Telephone Philadelphia in those days had very elaborate, once a year, a very elaborate show where they had dancing. It was in Atlantic City and it was really quite an elaborate, very fancy thing and she was always one of the dancers in the show and for years she had some of the costumes she had worn and that sort of thing.

Ms. Rogers: And she stopped working when you were born?

Ms. Burg: Theoretically, yes, though actually later on, during the Depression, she did work and after the Depression also. My father in 1929 or 30 really was kind of fed up with electrical engineering, might have even been 28, so he thought about going to medical school, it was probably before that. It was before my sister was born. He was accepted to medical school but was told that he needed one more year of Latin and he said no way, so he did not do it. And instead went into the laundry supply business with my uncle, my mother's brother. It was a wholesale laundry supply business which they had, supplying various laundries around Philadelphia and all the way down to Washington, and that continued until the Depression when things became so tight that it could only really support one family. So my father gave the business to my uncle. He tried to get back into engineering but was not successful, of course, in the early '30s, and so he did all sorts of things. He made jigsaw puzzles that were put into shoeboxes and sold, not sold, placed in drugstores and other places, because people were looking for things to do, just to occupy their time. I think they would rent for a penny a day, or something like that. He was always good with his hands. He made irons. I remember a number of these things as a young child. They were very good about insulating my sister and me. We never suffered from the depression at all. But they did, and in later years, we learned some more of those details. Like mother walking us to piano lessons and making a game of it. And then on the way home, stopping at a bakery and buying one piece of pastry for my sister and me to share because she "wasn't hungry." And many years later, she told us how she salivated as she watched us eating it. My father did many things just to occupy his time. Mother helped him count the pieces in the boxes of the puzzles and things of that type. He made my sister and me a gorgeous doll house which was a miniature, wooden very scaled copy of a house that appeared in *Good Housekeeping* or something, and we have it to this day. It was very elaborate. He ultimately wired it also, it had lights on it, and it's really a remarkable piece of workmanship. It's at my sister's house now because her grandchildren have been playing with it as they have grown up, and it really is quite a spectacular piece. The front and the back came off so we could get to all the rooms. He made a duplicate of their bedroom set for one of the bedrooms. My grandmother crocheted curtains for all the windows. Most of that stuff has been lost but the dollhouse itself still exists. It's quite a big thing. I guess its about three feet wide and two feet deep. My parents lost their home. They had bought a house in suburban Philadelphia when they were married. Actually they bought it before they were married. And my father came one day all excited with a handful of flowers that he had picked from the front lawn for my mother, which turned out to be dandelions. He didn't know one flower from the other. But during the Depression, they actually lost the house and moved to a rental house. Another reason that precipitated the move was for me to get to school, I had to cross a very major street in Philadelphia, Germantown Avenue, and they had guards there but one day, my mother at lunchtime, saw me walking down the street as she was wheeling my sister in a carriage down the street we lived on, which meant I had crossed the street by myself and they were very, very concerned about that. We moved to another area of Philadelphia where they rented a house but ultimately with the Depression, that even became impossible, and we moved into the home that my father's father had. Both grandfathers had died by that time, and my father, and we moved into the home where my grandmother and my uncle who was unmarried lived. He was taking care of her and running the shop, the store, which still existed. As a matter of fact, at that point they had opened a second store next to it which was ladies clothing and we lived with them which was extremely difficult. Again my sister and I didn't realize it, but it was not an easy situation. We were always shushed so we wouldn't wake my uncle who would sleep late, or things of that type, and my mother was made to feel that she was kind of there for their good graces, and then to answer your question, she did start working in the store at that time and worked part time. My grandmother worked all her life in the store. I mean she was a little lady, I'm built very much like her and very, obviously very bright, and she worked very hard, until ultimately the stores were shut. They weren't sold, they were shut but that was during World War II when my uncle went into service. We lived there until 1938. In about '37, my father, or '36, my father did get a job as a draftsman, not as an engineer, but as a draftsman. In 1938, he was able to get a job for the State of Pennsylvania, up in Selingsgove, Pennsylvania, which is about 50 miles north of Harrisburg, as the head engineer for inspection as they were building a new addition to the mental hospital. He lived there, I guess for about six or seven months while we were still in Philadelphia, and then we went up there for the summer with him. He told us stories about how toward the end of the summer having some politician come in and being shocked that he had gotten this job without going through the appropriate political hoops and was not "contributing to the political party." All the other people were. The man had walked into the office one day, the inspection office on the job, and told my father to get everybody in there and gave them a lecture that they weren't paying enough of their contributions, and then he asked my father "how did you ever get this job and you better start paying or else".

Ms. Rogers: I take it was from the Democratic Party at the time.

Ms. Burg: I'm not sure. I'm not sure. A lot of Pennsylvania was Republican at the time. He didn't know what he was going to do. He really didn't want to get involved with that kind of thing. And while he was worrying about it, just as a heaven opened up as one would say, a telegram arrived that same day offering him a job in Washington for the federal government as an electrical engineer. He went down and was interviewed and he got that job. Which was very good because my mother had told him she was never going to move back into the house with my grandmother and uncle whom we were very close to but you can imagine family things can get a little bit bad. So we all moved to Washington, DC in 1938. I was in junior high school. I was absolutely shocked to move to a segregated city. I never could really get over it. To me it was just absolutely horrifying. I had friends in Philadelphia of all colors. Not of all colors, because you didn't have quite the rainbow coalition you have today, but certainly the schools were integrated and I was in school with some of them and socialized a little bit with some of them, not a great deal because of where we lived. There was never a question in my mind that anything mattered in terms of color. And so it here it was.

Ms. Rogers: Beyond education, was the segregation obvious in aspects of life in Washington?

Ms. Burg: Oh yes, you'd go into Union Station. We would take a train. There were two different water fountains. There were two different sets of bathrooms. You'd get on a bus and all the blacks would go to the back. You'd go to a movie and they were in the balcony. It was a sleepy southern town in 1938 and a very, very segregated city. So yes, I found it very shocking. As matter a fact a few years later after things had started easing up, I remember a conversation, I guess I was about 14 at the time, with my piano teacher and her mother who were very strong segregationists and thought all of this was terrible and her mother looked at me very haughtily and said would you marry a black truck driver and, I think for a 14 year old, I gave her a very good answer: I said no, because I wouldn't marry a white one either. So, this was difficult for me adjusting in that regard. We lived in an apartment right off of 16th and Columbia Road and it was a lovely apartment, except it was small. My father's earnings were not that great as a government employee so my sister and I shared a room, which was really an enclosed porch and connected to my parents' bedroom as a matter of fact. But it was quite a nice experience after having lived with my grandmother. Oh in the summer in Selinsgrove, we were allowed to have all the pets that we had never been allowed to have in Philadelphia. So we had rabbits, we had a dog, we had cats, when we left, we gave the rabbits to our next door neighbors. A number of retired farmers lived there and professors at the Selinsgrove College. My sister and I cried and cried because when we gave the rabbits to our next door neighbor he thanked us profusely and said now he knew what they'd have for Thanksgiving Dinner. But we returned to Washington, of course, pet less, we couldn't bring the dog or the cats or anything into an apartment but we had had a good experience with it. I guess it was in that apartment my sister first began her activities in terms of her astronomy, and I think I told you I have a sister who is a world-renowned astronomer. She's received the Presidential Medal of Science, she's received just about every possible award short of the Nobel Prize and there are many people who feel that she should have received that had she, if she was not a woman, and maybe she will some day. As a matter of fact, last year, both the *USA Today* and other newspapers speculated that she would be the recipient but, of course, she was not.

Ms. Rogers: So what were you interested in at that time?

Ms. Burg: Medicine. Very much interested in medicine and science. My aunt gave me a chemistry set. I guess I was about ten years old. And I would use the microscope and was, our whole family, was really scientifically oriented and so there was never any question in my mind but that I was going to be a doctor. My parents were wonderful. They devoted most of their life to us and any interests we had, they would pursue and we would vacation together with them and I don't recall them every really going off on their own. In that regard it was always a family affair. I even remember for their anniversary in Philadelphia when we were young kids, they took us with them to a very nice restaurant when they could afford it we all went to some very famous supper club. I've forgotten now the name of the person who was appearing there and he signed autographs for us but we were included in what they did. Which is what you see a lot today in this generation. But I think in my generation, that was not done, you left your kids at home. So my main interest was science. And that is where I focused all my attention. In high school, we moved to 5th and Tuckerman. For those who know Washington, that was quite a dramatic move. But I had met a group of girls with whom I had become friendly and where everybody lived, and this was a very large Jewish area at the time, and so that was fine. My parents had looked at a house at 16th and Rittenhouse, and we objected strongly because it was far too far in the suburbs and we didn't want to be that isolated and so we ended up, we moved into a very small home at 5th and Tuckerman. It was within walking distance, actually it was a half of block from Coolidge High School. I continued on at Powell Junior High School which was near Columbia Road because I was in my last year and would go there everyday.

Ms. Rogers: How did you get there?

Ms. Burg: Walked a lot of the time or else took busses. The bus transportation was very good, I'd take a streetcar or a bus.

Ms. Rogers: And you did that alone?

Ms. Burg: Yeah. It was not considered unsafe or anything of that type. And so I continued. Then I enrolled at Coolidge. It was a brand new high school and ours was the first class that actually went through all three years. There too I primarily focused on science. I had a magnificent biology teacher and he was very helpful and helping. We did a lot of the projections and movies in the auditorium because he was in charge of that and I was on his VIP list so to speak. I had a perfectly normal growing up with my friends. We'd walk all over the place. We'd go to various movies and that sort of thing.

Ms. Rogers: Were things still segregated at that point in your high school years?

Ms. Burg: Yes. And as a matter of fact, growing up I was not the most popular girl on the block. I had lots of girlfriends. Very few boyfriends. I had a couple of boyfriends. But not that much. Normally, things were segregated – not in terms of color. I think there was kind of a bifurcation into groups. We had a large Catholic group, and a large Jewish group and each kind of kept to ourselves, socially, and that sort of thing. We would, of course, have no problems with classes, but there was just kind of a division that I don't think you would find today.

Ms. Rogers: Was there overt anti-Semitism? Did you ever hear slurs of any kind?

Ms. Burg: Not at that point. Heard them when I was much younger in Philadelphia. I was accused of being a Christ-killer by my girlfriend across the street who was also age 5, 6 or 7. So you knew it had to come from the home or something of that kind. It really didn't bother me that much at that point. I think we were aware of it. You've got to remember this was in the late 30's, early 40's when things were going bad in Europe and the beginning of World War II and so certainly we were aware of anti-Semitism being a problem. I never really met it, overtly at least. Whether I met it with some of my teachers and didn't realize it, I don't know. I certainly had no difficulty in terms of high school. I graduated as valedictorian in the class, so I don't think there was a lot of focus that would have impacted on my courses or anything of that type. I just wasn't really aware of it at that juncture. Maybe I was naïve. I don't think it was quite as overt in those days. We knew about Father Coughlin and we knew about and we were concerned about that sort of thing but we were not really involved in worrying about all of that. So high school years were fun years.

Ms. Rogers: Did you still plan to be a doctor at the time you graduated?

Ms. Burg: Oh yes. I had wanted to go to Radcliffe, and I think I would have had no difficulty getting into Radcliffe. I never went through with the application because this was 1943 and there was a great fear, especially in Washington, of being bombed and that sort of thing from the war, from World War II. My father was an air raid warden of the area and he was terribly concerned that his "little girl," (and I remained his little girl even when I was fifty) might get stuck in Boston if there was problems on the East Coast because of the war and be completely isolated and cut off from the family. Also, as valedictorian I received a full tuition scholarship to George Washington University. In those days George Washington University gave scholarships to the valedictorian of the class of each of the high schools in Washington. So here I had the full tuition scholarship at GW. My father I think was earning $3,000 a year in those days which was considered a fairly good upper median salary and I knew I wanted to go to medical school and that would be a tremendous expense to him; and so I felt I just couldn't turn down a full scholarship. So I went to George Washington University, lived at home, went by bus and streetcar every day. If I had night classes, my father would walk the block and a half to where I would get off the bus on my way home and be standing there waiting for me to get home. We had a car, a used car that he bought after the Depression. It was a small car. We had a garage in our house which I said was a very small house and the car was taken out on Sundays for trips. We'd take a ride into the country up to Rockville, going up on Georgia Avenue and back on Wisconsin Avenue or vice versa, being in the country most of the time. Otherwise, anyplace we went by streetcar or by bus. You walked to the grocery store. There was no question that this was the way to do it. It was fine. That was the advantage of growing up in the city. So I went to GW, I majored in chemistry and pre-med. I had a pre-med advisor who kept telling me how I shouldn't be a doctor. I did what in retrospect was a very foolish thing. Again I was in a hurry.

It was World War II. There was social life because I did join a sorority and I was very active in the sorority. It was known as a Jewish sorority but actually had been founded, and that was why I was interested in it, many years earlier at Hunter College when some of the non-Jewish freshmen had discovered that their Jewish friends could not get into a sorority with them and so they founded a nonsectarian sorority, and this was the first major nonsectarian sorority that ever existed and therefore I found it of interest and was willing to join it and became quite active in it. So I did have social life. But it was a different atmosphere. I remember one of our pledge class songs was "You're Either Too Young Or Too Old" and it was a parody on a song known at the time, but was about the boys that were around.

Ms. Rogers: Because of the war?

Ms. Burg: We did not have too many of the Army and Navy students, the V-12 or whatever it was called where there were actually people in the military who were being trained in college. Being as short as I am and, since this is on tape, I guess I better say I am proud of being 5 foot and 1/2 inch. It seemed the only boys who were around who were interested in me were well over 6 feet whereas one of my sorority sisters who was 5' 7", the only boys who were interested in her were about 5'2". So we had lots of time joking and laughing about that. We had some social life but I decided to do college in a little over two years because I was anxious to go to medical school and so I did, it was kind of crazy in retrospect. I was a lab assistant in the chemistry department because they learned I could type. I had had a job when I was in high school. In those days the Government was open on Saturdays for half a day. So I got a job as a typist on Saturdays working for the Department of Agriculture which many years later I discovered was still on my record and counted toward retirement. It was kind of strange seeing my handwritten application for the position.

Ms. Rogers: It was part of your federal employment record.

Ms. Burg: I was very impressed. As a matter of fact, when I looked at my records, they even had my application in my handwriting, so when people talk about the mess of the Federal government, some things they manage to apparently keep track of. In any event, I did all of the typing for the GW chemistry department which meant I typed all of the tests and exams and boy was I offered lots of money by people

Ms. Rogers: To preview the exams.

Ms. Burg: To see the exams. Never took any of it. But I had a key to the lab so the reason I was really able to do all my labs was they allowed me to go in off hours and do them. So I was able to do all of that. But my zoology prof came up to me and said had I applied to med school yet. This was the same man who kept telling me I shouldn't go.

Ms. Rogers: And why did he tell you shouldn't go?

Ms. Burg: I don't know whether it was that he was opposed to women, whether he was anti-Semitic, because I did begin to meet it a lot at that point or what the story was. But he just kept saying I would not be a good doctor. I would never get into medical school and so I had figured I would wait a year and apply to a number of medical schools to see what happened. Because I had very good grades. I paid a price, I think, for pushing through as much as I did. I missed *Phi Beta Kappa* by about a thousandth of a point or something like that, part of which was because I didn't cross my legs properly in my logic class and he gave me a C, which I think was the only C I got. You're making faces, but I remember he left school abruptly when I was taking a second logic course because apparently he was having an affair with one of his students whose husband was in the military and came home and found out about it and we suddenly had the President of the University in there teaching our class. My zoology professor came up to me and he said, have you applied to medical school? And I said no. And he said, Well you know, the cutoff is tomorrow, you better get your application in. Well I took this as a signal that he maybe he had changed his mind and I rushed and got an application. This was an advanced zoology class, he taught comparative anatomy. He bet me a milkshake that I would get into medical school. Since he was he one that had to approve it, I thought this was a pretty good indication I would be admitted. He had previously said to me that he saw I had a great interest in science and if I would like to come up to his office some day, he would be happy to paint all the location of my organs on my body, which, of course, scared me to death. You've got to realize, this is 43, I was what 17 or 18 years old and I didn't want to get anywhere near that man. I was admitted to medical school and that was a fun story because the day I got the letter, I had had my eyes examined, my pupils were dilated and I came home to find the letter there and I could make out that the letter was from the medical school but I of course couldn't read it. I was going crazy until my mother came home and could read it for me. She said, yes I had been admitted to the class.

Ms. Rogers: So this was GW Medical School?

Ms. Burg: This was GW Medical School.

Ms. Rogers: And you at that point had not applied anywhere else?

Ms. Burg: No, no, as I said, I really thought I would wait a year because this was in I guess probably in the fall and I don't really recall, but they would have notified us I guess by the spring whether we were in or not and so, by that time, had not really graduated from college yet. And as a matter of fact, I got my degree after the first year of medical school, during the fall of medical school. As a matter of fact, the University gave me a problem. They said I didn't have enough non-science courses and I was smart enough to argue with them and tell them, look, I took all the required pre-med, all the required courses I needed for my chemistry major. Where could I have worked those in? So they waived them for me and I got my Bachelor of Science degree, I guess in the fall of '45 having entered in '43, so it was a very foolish thing to have done in retrospect, but I did it. I completed my first year of medical school, George Washington Medical School. I met my first husband in the summer of '45 and entered school in the fall of '45 and so, that was an interesting thing. He was 9 years older than I was, he was from Germany, his parents had sent him out to avoid the holocaust. He had been in school in Switzerland for a number of years and had come here in 1937 and in 1938, had gotten a job working for the Hecht Company and when I met him, he had worked up to be the youngest buyer they had ever had. But he had always wanted to go back to school but couldn't afford it because he was self-supporting. His parents, my father-in-law was in Buchenwald but managed to get out in late '37 because in those days you could get out of Germany if you had a visa to some other country. You could not get it to the United States, but my father-in-law's youngest brother had been here since 1928 working for the federal government, had some good connections and was able to get the family a visa into Luxembourg where they stayed for a year, and then finally their number came up to come to the United States and they were literally on the water four hours when Germany and England declared war or they would have never gotten out. We wanted to get married. There were 10 women in our class of about 170 in my med school class, and I did meet some anti-Semitism there. My anatomy professor who I didn't recognize at the time, but ultimately realized in later years, was gay and very anti-Semitic. That was obvious because the person sitting next to me was another woman who has remained a friend of mine for all these years. Her name was Cohen, but she had been brought up as a Lutheran. Her mother was not Jewish, and one day when we were getting our exams back, the so-called blue books, and he was calling names, my maiden name being Cooper, I sat next to June Cohen, and he said Cooper and I held out my hand and, it became one of these real Alphonse and Gaston routines. I held out my hand and he pulled the blue book back. I'd hold out my hand. And finally he blurted out, I thought you were Cohen. He tried to bump me out of med school because I was ill one day and we had an exam. He had a rule that if you have an exam and you missed it, he was a real sadist. But if you missed it, you ended up with a "C", but you could take another examination, but you had to have a doctor's excuse. So I did miss the exam. I was running a high fever. I went to the doctor. Got the excuse from the doctor. I brought it in and took it into him. He wasn't even teaching that class, but he was the head of the anatomy department, and he looked at me and he said "there will be no makeup exam given." And I said what? This was one of three exams and I had a zero on one of three exams which can be pretty horrendous in those days or on any day. Everybody was shocked.

Ms. Rogers: He said this in front of the whole .....

Ms. Burg: No, he said this in front of the other professor, the assistant professor who was teaching the course—it was a course in neuro-anatomy--and he really was very adamant about it. And I said to him, what did you say sir? Because in those days you didn't go to the Dean or anything and so everybody was absolutely shocked. Each year, he would move into the rooming house where some of the male students were living, and that night they were all talking about this because the whole class was just horrified and looked up and he was there and the people who were living in the rooming house all flunked their next exam. I tell you, he was a real sadist. He slipped on the ice that winter and broke his arm and everybody said that Max, my first husband, at that point, my boyfriend, must have pushed him because he would walk over every day and meet me at lunch time and we'd have lunch together. The only other time we would see each other was on the weekends because I was just too busy with my classes. During that year, we became engaged. We wanted to get married and it was very unusual for a woman to go to medical school married, so I asked for a leave of absence. When we went through my father's papers after he died, I found a letter that the med school had sent to him, not to me, but to him, saying that they were granting me a two-year leave of absence even though that was very unusual, but since I was such an outstanding student in the class that they were willing to do it.

Ms. Rogers: Were you still living at home at that time?

Ms. Burg: Yes, we had moved though. We were now living in southeast Washington because after the war, there was a tremendous need for housing and what you found was someone else would buy a house, and those people would have to vacate, then somebody else would buy a house, and they would have to vacate, and our house was sold and my parents did not feel it was something they wanted to or could afford to buy. So we ended up in some housing, in apartments that were being built, in southeast Washington. Mother worked there because my sister knew the daughter of the people who were building so that's how we got in. The woman who was the resident manager asked mother to work as her assistant. You asked if mother worked. She worked there doing bookkeeping and that sort of thing. I took a bus every day to medical school from there. No difficulty. I didn't think that I should have a car and drive or anything of thatsort.

Ms. Rogers: And that neighborhood at that time was racially integrated because now it's pretty much all African-American

Ms. Burg: Now it's pretty much all African-American. And in those days it wasn't really wasn't racial, it was a whole new development, and what you found was a lot of young or middle-aged Jewish people who for some reason seemed to congregate there. There was no objection to racial integration. But it was just not the thing. It was years later before you began to see communities become racially integrated. So this was all white. It was a very safe area. You didn't really see any racial integration there at all. So we married in December of '46 and I spent two years trying to decide what I wanted to do. In the meantime, my husband had gone back to school on the GI bill. We lived on $110 a month or something like and our rent was $90. It was an interesting time of our lives. We had been able to get an apartment, again because mother was working there since there was a long waiting list. So we lived down the street from my parents. Mother talked about remembering--she remembered it more than I did--I would watch for sales, when there was a meat sale, I would buy a piece of steak and cut it into certain portions and that was the most we could have that night and the pieces were individually frozen and that sort of thing. My husband had a part-time job. We managed.

Ms. Rogers: But you had no job at that point?

Ms. Burg: No, that's no true. When I left school, I began to work for the Naval Research Laboratory which was in southeast Washington. I got a job in the library, abstracting and indexing the Manhattan Papers which was really a quite an interesting thing.

Ms. Rogers: Did you have to get a security clearance?

Ms. Burg: Yes, I had a security clearance. Not only did I have security clearance, I was one of the two people who was involved with making sure that everything was locked up every night and we had hundreds of file cabinets with four drawers in each one of them and the guards would go through and try each drawer and if, God forbid, you had not caught one of them, the next morning, there would be a notice of security breach on your desk and you would be called on the carpet to account for it. Even though many of these documents by that time had been declassified. There were some that were still classified but many of them were not, but they weren't stamped so everything had to be treated as very highly classified material. It's what made me hate classified material to a point that when I was on the bench and, of course, faced with many instances where material, facts would be classified, I would make the parties go through every possible extreme before we had to introduce those classified documents into evidence and I tried to avoid it like the plague. I often was successful in doing so, but at times was not. But no, it was not fun. I did that, and then when Max, I guess Max graduated in 1947 or something and finally got a job. It was very difficult in those days. He got a job as a junior accountant and I had always known I wanted to go back to school, and I debated for two years whether I wanted to go to back to med school or not, and it was a decision he said I had to make by myself. He was not going to participate. I finally decided that I would not go back. There was not a university in Washington where I felt there was a good enough department that I could take a graduate degree in biochemistry or physiology, which would have been one of my choices because I liked those. I was not completely thrilled with medicine. Of course, I wasn't really exposed to what would term real medicine, but the little bits I had of it, I found that I didn't enjoy that much. I always said if I couldn't get to medical school, I would go to law school, so I decided to apply to law school. And I applied to law school and I applied to George Washington University Law School because, I guess Catholic would have, but Georgetown did not accept women in those days.

Ms. Rogers: Did you know anybody who was in law school or did you know any lawyers while you were growing up?

Ms. Burg: No.

Ms. Rogers: It came out of nowhere?

Ms. Burg: I guess it was more than out of nowhere. You know Jewish children as they grew up either became a doctor or a lawyer. And I liked some of the social action aspects that some lawyers seemed to be involved in. I had gotten involved. I guess it was later when I became involved with B'nai Brith and the Anti-Defamation League and things of that sort. But I had always been interested in human rights possibly because of the Holocaust and things of that type and law seemed to be a good vehicle in which to get involved in all of that. But, no members of the family had been lawyers. I don't know that we had any family friends who were lawyers. They were mostly scientists and engineers or business people and so I applied to GW Law School and I was accepted. In those days there wasn't such a thing as LCATs or anything of that sort. And I went to school at night. Before I went to law school I did decide I'd better take an exam, a psychological test to see if this was good for me because I had given up medicine and I didn't want to get into another area that I was not going to be happy with. And so I went to GW's Department of Psychology, I guess it was, and took a whole series of aptitude tests.

Ms. Rogers: And I imagine that was pretty unusual at the time too.

Ms. Burg: So really in retrospect, a little foolish because if you're at all intelligent, you can slant the answers anyway you really wanted to. At least the tests I was given, you can slant the answers pretty much anyway you really wanted to, and so I took this whole battery of tests on a number of Saturdays and of course, it came out with law being at the top, science and medicine being quite high. The one that was D--they ranked them A, B, C and D. The one that was D was being a housewife. And that didn't surprise me because there was no doubt in my mind about that. I should say that my parents were very unusual for their time. They brought their daughters up to believe they could do anything they wanted. I mean we did not know there was such a thing that women didn't do this or women didn't do that. Part of it, there was no question but that we were to go to college, my father had an older sister who had married and her husband had deserted her with a six-month old child. She had had to move home and he said that was never going to happen to his daughters. They would always be able to stand on their own two feet and in later years when my parents said both my sister and I were working too hard, we'd tell them it was their fault. They had brought us up that we should do this, and what did they expect us to do with it? It was all said in a very loving, joking way. And so I went to law school atnight. Again, never thought of asking my parents for help for it financially. Just didn't seem the right thing to do. They were not really in a position where that was something they could do very easily. And so we,

Ms. Rogers: Was you father still working at the time at that point though?

Ms. Burg: O yeah, Father was still working. Still for the federal government, Department of the Navy. And so, I. There was one scholarship at GW for which I applied and I did not get it. Nobody got it. I found out subsequently it had not been awarded for a number of years. I always thought if I were ever in a position where I could create a scholarship, it would be mandatory that they find somebody to give it to every year. But I did start working for some of the law school professors when they learned indexing and abstracting was my job. A couple of them were writing textbooks and employed me at $1.00 an hour to index their books for them. And at the end of the first year, or first semester, I decided that it was just too hard to try to do law school and work full time. And so I at that juncture, I did quit my job and become a full-time student.

Ms. Rogers: And the full time work was all for law professors. So you were basically….

Ms. Burg: Oh no, no, no. That was very part-time.

Ms. Rogers: But the full time work you were doing.

Ms. Burg: Was at the Navy. I still had this job at the Naval Research Lab and so I left that and went back to law school full time. And at the end of my first year, the scholarship again became available, and one of the profs said to me are you applying, and I said I don't think it's worth it. They said I think you should. I think because they had gotten to know me, I was not an unknown quantity. I did get the scholarship. So my last two years at the law school were on scholarship, which made our lives much easier. Books were still terribly expensive, but at least I had the tuition, and I had a few dollars, very few from indexing the books with the profs. I took some graduate courses. In those days you had the choice of an LLB or a JD. Now it's all JD. And in order to get a JD, you had to take some postgraduate courses. So I did that, so I took some in taxation because with my husband now a CPA, I decided that I would like to major in federal taxation and with my interest in math which had always been very strong, I liked all of the cost aspects and that sort of thing working with figures.

Ms. Rogers: So these were graduate courses in the law school?

Ms. Burg: Yes, in the law school. You had to take, I forget whether it was one, two or three graduate courses in order to get a JD. Ultimately now, of course, everybody gets a JD and even those people who got a LLB I think could have it converted to a JD. But in those days, both degrees were given. I was on Law Review, and there I did meet some anti-Semitism, I believe, because I should have been editor of the Law Review. I was first in the class, but through some machinations, the professor who was the faculty advisor, made someone else the editor-in-chief and I was made taxation editor, which was fine. We all worked together so it was okay. It wasn't okay, I was annoyed about it, but there wasn't a lot I could do about it.

Ms. Rogers: Was it ever said why that happened? You surmised that?

Ms. Burg: No. It was never said. Things weren't that overt, but I really feel from that and other things that happened and knowing the man who was involved in it was that, since the other person who was appointed was a woman, so it could not have been anti-feminism.

Ms. Rogers: You mean the editor-in-chief was a woman that year?

Ms. Burg: The editor-in-chief was a woman.

Ms. Rogers: Had that ever happened before?

Ms. Burg: I don't think so. I'm not sure. But, no it was a woman, so it couldn't have been anti-feminine thing, but he looked at certain, he did certain machinations with the grade points and it was all supposed to be done on one's point count. She and I were very close, I mean she and I were good friends. I was very pleased with her doing it. She was from New Mexico and ultimately went to Alaska and everybody lost track of her. We don't really know what happened to her.

Ms. Rogers: What percentage of your class was female?

Ms. Burg: Very little. I guess there were about a dozen of us in the class and it was a very large class. I guess I could find out by asking GW and if you like, I could fill in those figures. It was a large class because it was a class that entered in '48 and this was post World War II so an awful lot of the people who had come back were in the class on the GI Bill and that sort of thing, so it was a huge class.

Ms. Rogers: Huge like 400.

Ms. Burg: Like 300 to 400, some place around there. The women were all really some of the top people in the class. A number of us were law review editors, I mean. Its true today in different ways, but in order to succeed you still have to be a little bit better than the men against whom you are competing. I made a few friends in law school but I didn't do that much socializing. I was married. A number of us were married, so there were a few friends and some of them I still see to this day or know to this day. Several of the women became judges,.

Ms. Rogers: Of the women, were most of them roughly your contemporaries? If I were to count, it sounds as if by that time you probably were the age that most people were in law school.

Ms. Burg: They were mostly my contemporaries. Maybe even a few years older than I was, because many of them had done other things before they went to law school also. In that regard, it was still a novelty to have women in law school. There were enough that there was a law sorority and it was fairly active and I was asked to join it. I did. I learned several years later the sorority constitution had a discriminatory clause in it. I was absolutely shocked to learn that. It was open to white Christian women, but you could get an exception and apparently they had applied for an exception for me without telling me, and so I wrote a very strong letter of resignation which was not honored because they were still trying to get women to join in later years touting the fact that I had graduated first in the class. So I wrote another very strong letter saying I wanted to no longer be associated in any manner, form, or name with them. I found this all out because one of the women who was active in the sorority had gone to the national meeting and said there had been an effort to remove the discriminatory clause. Of course, my ears immediately perked up, since she said that it had been defeated by one vote. So I asked about it. It turned out afterwards it hadn't been defeated by one vote. She was not very good at counting. If there had been one more, there would have been a third voting for it instead of against it. They asked me to stay in because "next year, we'll see that it goes through and you people always want others fighting your fight for you and you should stay in and fight for yourself". So I stayed in for one more year. This was all in law school and then the next year when I really found out what the numbers were is when I sent in my letter of resignation because it again did not pass. I suspect today, of course, it has, but who knows. I can't imagine that a discriminatory clause would exist anymore.

Ms. Rogers: Did you see yourself as a vocal advocate in those days? Somebody who really stood up for herself in general. Or did you try to fade into the woodwork, or something in between?

Ms. Burg: I wanted to be one of the boys. Really, you weren't the advocate for feminism that you would see today. You had to get along with your male contemporaries, and you did it by not standing out. I had some experiences subsequently which we will get to when I was clerking where again you didn't push yourself forward. You waited for them to approach you, most of the people who I socialized with in the law school were other women. There were one or two men who I became very friendly with. One of whom I was a year behind him in law school married a woman in my class and I became friendly with both of them. She ultimately became a district court judge here and he died at a relatively young age compared to the rest of us. But, as I say I did very little socializing. First of all you worked awfully hard in law school. You know that. There wasn't a lot of time for socializing and the time that existed, I was married, I wanted to be with my husband. We had our friends, our social group from that type of group and I was still very friendly with some of the girls I had grown up with in Washington. As we all had gotten married, we had been bridesmaids at one another's weddings and we still saw each other and once a month we'd get together and have a splurge and go out to dinner, not to a very expensive restaurant, but it was all any of us could afford at the time and we would go out and do non-expensive things like museums or hiking and that sort of thing.

Ms. Rogers: Did those girls all end up going to college?

Ms. Burg: Yes, all the ones I grew up with and are friendly with today all went to college, but most of them did not go on professionally, their undergraduate degrees were more of an academic nature. Some of them continued to work. One of my closest friends worked until a few years ago but it was more in the teaching end and that sort of thing, counseling and psychology. Many of them took time off when their children were young and then went back to it. Really, we all married very young, we all were extremely young when we married. I admire the women of today who learn to live. I never had an opportunity in my life to live only for me. I went from living with my parents to living with my husband. When my first husband died, I had two young children whom I had to be concerned about. When I remarried, I married a widower, we had four teenage children so I never in my life had the opportunity which I saw that my daughters have, which was to really only be concerned about themselves. To live for themselves. I think it's a wonderful experience. One that I was never able to have. And so, most of them that I am friendly with today all went on for college and that sort of thing. Again there was no question, but again we came from that Jewish group where education was considered very important. I had lunch yesterday with a woman in my field who is very, very good, outstanding, and she came from a different background. She said her father was an immigrant from Greece and the sons all went to college, but the daughters were not educated, and she took it upon herself to contact her congressman and get the application to attend the Air Force Academy and her parents didn't know any of this until after she had been accepted. And that wouldn't have happened in the group that I grew up with, where education was considered very important, regardless of the sex of the child. And so, I think it's just a different type of atmosphere.

Ms. Rogers: So, I diverted you. You were talking about your social life during law school and being a young married.

Ms. Burg: So, we did interesting, we did that type of thing. Along the way, we decided it was time to maybe start considering a family, and I ran into great difficulties on that score. I don't know whether you want to know my whole gory history of that but I did have 14 miscarriages along theline.

Ms. Rogers: Was that all during law school?

Ms. Burg: No, some of them were during law school. You had askedwhether my miscarriages were in law school. Some of them were. Some of them we never knew, it was so early. I had purposely gone to a doctor who did not believe in drugs which was just as well because if that had not been the case when I ultimately did have my daughter, it would have been during the days when the drugs had resulted in what is DES. I'm grateful that was not the case. You asked whether it was during when I was in law school. Certainly I was in the midst of a miscarriage in my finals in my final year of law school and it impacted somewhat on my exams. There is no doubt about it because I did not do as well for many reasons in those exams as I had in the others up to that time. While I didn't socialize in law school, there were a lot of people, because of the fact that I was doing well grade-wise, who always wanted to study with me and we spent a lot of time in those days - very few places in those days were air-conditioned - we spent a lot of time at the Library of Congress in the Jefferson Building because it was one of the few air-conditioned places and then we'd go all the way upstairs to the top roof, kind of attic room where we would talk when we weren't studying and we'd discuss the cases that were coming up for the exam and everybody, these were all men, they'd all be quoting case after case and I wouldn't remember case names. To this day, I don't remember case names very well, but when we'd take the exams, they would get Bs and Cs and I would get the As because I was able to reason as you do in law school from a set of facts to a result. It's not very important to remember the names of the cases, you can always find those out, but it is helpful to be able to use appropriate reasoning. I guess it was in the early spring of my last year, which was the spring of 1950, the Dean called me in and told me I was graduating first in the class and I would receive the John Bell Larner Award and this was before I took all the exams so I kept saying to my husband, what will happen if I don't do well, and of course the pressure of that plus the fact that I was going through a miscarriage didn't help very much and some of my grades did go down, but not enough to knock me out of first place in the class.

Ms. Rogers: I want to get a sense of the years again. I thought you had said you started in 48.

Ms. Burg: I went through thesummer.

Ms. Rogers: So you started part-time in 48.

Ms. Burg: I started one semester at night in 48 and then I don't believe it was the fall of '47, I think it was the spring of '48, but summer classes were still going. Remember this was post-World War II and there were a lot of people who had come back who were anxious to get on with their lives so the classes went through the summer as well as the year and I just took heavy schedules throughout so that I finished in June 1950.

Ms. Rogers: So that erases one of my questions which was, did you do summer clerkships or work at law firms or anything like that?

Ms. Burg: No. That was not quite as popular in those days. No, we were in class the whole time. So then, from a personal aspect, of course, emotionally all of this was extremely difficult for me. But ultimately I did graduate first in the class and I think I told you this story, but I guess you want it on tape. The Dean called me in and said that normally they would find a good position or a good clerkship for their first in the class graduate, but did I realize that in this case, that was not possible. And as I speak to young women these days, I say I don't know whether to be more shocked that he said it or that I agreed with him but I did agree with him. I understood that. He said they would be very willing and glad to write a letter of recommendation for any position for which I was applying and made no effort whatsoever to find anything for me.

Ms. Rogers: Now you said "in this case," they couldn't do it because you were female.

Ms. Burg: Yes. Because I was a woman. And I, in retrospect, maybe should have been shocked, but I was not. It was just a different time. One of the women college sorority sisters of mine who was older than I and who was an attorney and who had very good political connections because of her family connections, was horrified when she heard this, and so she used some of her connections and, since I was interested in taxation, she inquired or I had inquired and found out that there were three new tax court judges who had just been appointed or confirmed by the Senate and through her political connections, I was instructed to send my CV and my resume and any letters of recommendation to these three judges, which I did. I guess I should back up because, the day before graduation, there was a very elaborate tea at George Washington and I was given the John Bell Larner Medal for having graduated first in the class. The President of the University, Cloyd Heck Marvin, presented the award and when he looked down and started saying my name, and saw I was a woman, he began stuttering so he could not get it out. After the ceremony, the PR person from GW rushed up to me and said to me, please don't leave, and I was interviewed by a number of newspapers because they had decided it would make a very good story to have an article about the first woman ever to graduate first in the class at GW Law School. Again, in retrospect, I was naïve because when I was interviewed, they asked me what I was going to do. It didn't occur to me to say I don't know because they haven't helped me find a position, I said I was tired - I didn't tell them I had just undergone a miscarriage - and I was going to take the summer off, then I would study for the Bar and then I would look for something in the fall. The next day, this hit the front page of the local section of the Washington papers and my family rushed out and bought copies, so did I. My photograph was there with the Dean of the Law School and the President of the University, etc. etc. I did include that in the resumes that I sent to these various judges. Then in the fall one of them called me. The other two did not. One of them called me and asked me to come in for an interview and he said he wasn't sure if he had a position or not. In those days, the tax court had, did not have law clerks as such. What they had were attorney-advisors and they stayed on for years. They stayed on sometimes until they were eligible for retirement so that in many ways, some of these men, because it was all men at that point, were more knowledgeable about tax law than the judges who were appointed, so often when the judges were appointed, they would take one of these attorney-advisors as their attorney-advisor and each judge had two of them, with the exception of the chief judge who had three. There was one woman tax court judge in those days, Marion Harron. She was not someone who I think made the life of women following after her easier. She had had a rough time, but she had a terrible reputation as a judge. As a matter fact, tax court judge is a 15-year term, there was a lot of opposition to her reappointment and it became a real feminist thing involving even Eleanor Roosevelt who finally persuaded, took a strong role in it, and she was reappointed. She had interviewed me because she had a vacancy but she did not offer me a position and what I didn't realize until afterwards, when Steve Rice said he didn't know if he had a position, there were two attorney-advisors for the judge whom he was succeeding who had died. And he was not sure whether both of them were going to be available and if so he had said he would take them. Both of them were men who had many years' experience and had children in college and he had felt that it was not right for them to suddenly be without a position. But what I didn't know until afterwards is that the woman judge had asked for one of these two men because she wanted a senior person and the less senior of the two, you've got to remember neither one of them was young, was the one who was assigned to her which opened up a space for me. My husband and I became friendly with Steve Rice and his wife. He had been the legislative counsel of the Senate and had been an Annapolis graduate and had gone back during World War II to become an officer of the Navy in charge of, he didn't fly any more but he was in charge of the planes on a major aircraft carrier. He was up on the bridge when a Kamikaze plane came in so he ended up with a badly shattered leg. He spent many, many months in the hospital as they reconstructed it. He was fine ultimately, but the pressures of being legislative counsel of the Senate were pretty great and he decided it would be nicer to be a judge so he had contacts. Anyway he was nominated and confirmed as a judge of the tax court and Lee, his wife, used to tell me he walked around the house before he offered me the position saying, "she's got a wonderful record, never had a woman attorney work for me before, she's got a wonderful record, never had a woman attorney work for me before." There had never been a woman I don't think. I have heard more recently there might have been one woman before me but there certainly was not when I got there.

Ms. Rogers: In the attorney-advisor position.

Ms. Burg: In the attorney-advisor position. So he offered it to me. As luck would have it, of course, he kept one of these two very senior people on as his number 1 and I was his number 2 attorney-advisor. And the number 1 one didn't want a woman in his office with him. He had enough seniority that he could have a private office. So as luck would have it, I was put in the office with the one who had been his number 2 attorney and who was now working for the woman judge. Marian Harron. So I was in the office with him. We shared the office. He never really became very friendly. We talked a little bit, but certainly not roommates in any sense of the word and part of that was because of the fact that shortly after I came to the court, she decided she didn't want him as her attorney-advisor any more and she wanted him to be fired. And here he was with two kids in college and a very soft-spoken quiet man to begin with, but certainly not terribly happy about it, as were none of the other male attorney-advisors there, which there were about twenty-five or thirty and here I am the young kid on the block who's taking his job, which was not true, but that's how it was looked upon because but for the fact that he had been assigned to her, he would have had the job, and so when you asked me earlier did you take kind of a quiet role, I found the best thing to do under the circumstances was to take a very quiet role. And I did. I never went down to have coffee with everybody unless I was asked. I never had lunch with them unless I was asked. I never initiated any of it.

Ms. Rogers: And were you asked?

Ms. Burg: Once in a very rare, rare while. And, fine, I was married, I had my own social group, I had my own activities outside, but it was a very tense situation until one of the other judges decided to take him on as his attorney-advisor which solved that problem but still there was already the ground work plus I am sure a certain amount of on the part of some of them not being happy to see a woman in there. I never became friendly enough with them to really know. I became very friendly with the judge and sometimes we would go to lunch together but only if he had, when we would finish a case, and then it was very interesting. I didn't realize it at the time, he was really an alcoholic. I mean he could drink a bottle of bourbon in an evening and not show any of it. But we would go out for lunch and his lunch would consist of 9 double Gibsons and a bowl of vichyssoise. He took me up to the Hill a couple of times when he was visiting former colleagues. One of the things the other judges wanted him to do was to get a good retirement system for the tax court judges which didn't exist at the time and so he, with his contacts up there, was ultimately able to get one where they get the same retirement as district court judges which is full salary, etc. after a certain period of time. So he was up lobbying for that. He'd take me up to the Hill and we'd sit around with some of the other people and have, they'd all have their couple of martinis and, of course, big shot me who had never drunk anything in her life, but they'd insist so I would have a martini, and I'd nurse it as carefully as I could and they would all be drinking away and ultimately, they'd insist I have another one, and I'd end up sick as a dog and really for years thereafter, I couldn't look at anything like that. But most of the time, I worked very hard.

Ms. Rogers: So your other counterpart, the other person who worked for him who was much more senior. Did you have much of a relationship with him?

Ms. Burg: Just professionally.

Ms. Rogers: He was the one who didn't want to share office space with you.

Ms. Burg: I don't think he resented me as such, he liked to smoke cigars and so I'm just as happy I was not in his office. Of course, I was a smoker in those days too, but not cigars, and professionally, we got along very well. He taught me a great deal. I mean there was no problems there at all and, all of that was very, very. I mean I was there for 2 1/2 years. It was a very good learning experience.

Ms. Rogers: Were you still having miscarriages?

Ms. Burg: Still having miscarriages. Well, but at that point, I had stopped being able to conceive at all so I was going, a little later than that I was going through all sorts of treatments. And then ultimately, they decided that even surgery wouldn't help me so we began seriously trying to adopt, and I left the court in 1953. As I say it was a marvelous experience. I learned a lot. I don't know whether I should go into the fact because I've already named names, but when I would travel with the judge at times to act as his law clerk you know his clerk of court, once or twice he made very serious sexual advances--not very pleasant. It was after he had had a lot to drink. And again, I kind of had to overlook it, but during the Thomas interviews, I could relive a lot of that a great deal because I could relate to what she was saying. And, he didn't, I mean the fact that I refused the advances did not affect how he, our relationship. You know, from his viewpoint either. I don't know whether I did it right or not, but I played it cool and made it clear I was not at all interested and please just take your hands off.

Ms. Rogers: And then you moved on.

Ms. Burg: And we moved on.

Ms. Rogers: Was that something that played a part in your leaving at 2 1/2 years?

Ms. Burg: No, not at all. The one or two episodes that happened much earlier on. When he knew what the limits were he became very respectful of them. Even when he had a lot to drink.

Ms. Rogers: What did prompt you to decide to move on?

Ms. Burg: Well, I had never thought of it as a lifetime job. I had looked at it more as a clerking thing. The doctor thought maybe if I stopped working under such pressures, I would be able to conceive. So I guess at that point, there was some hope that I could conceive. I think I would have left. I thought it was time to move on. I inquired at the Department of Justice but in those days, the Tax Division didn't hire women and so I started practicing law on my own. I specialized in tax, I became quite successful in it. It was a local practice.

Ms. Rogers: You rented out the space somewhere?

Ms. Burg: No, first I worked out of home. Remember my husband was a CPA. Ultimately, he went out on his own, so I used to say, I have office space. I would just use his office, and I would jokingly say that he wouldn't evict me if I couldn't pay the rent.. I worked at home or I worked down in his office. I got a lot of referrals from CPAs and I was very good at what I was doing. I did have space with a tax lawyer for a time but that did not work out.

Ms. Rogers: And the situations were generally people called in for audits or what?

Ms. Burg: No, this was advice. In Washington, DC there were two types of tax practices, one would have been a national type of practice and the other was primarily local business people. The local business people who were primarily in need of tax advice were the builders because Washington is not a commercial area as such. Building was quite active in those days. So I ended up working with a number of the builders here in town and, in retrospect, had a nice roster of some of the ones whom I worked with. Often we met in the office of the CPAs because that is where all the records would be, etc. It was always fun to me to see the point where they stopped looking at me as a little girl and suddenly started listening to me and you could sense when this occurred in the course of the meeting. Only once did I use the fact that I was a woman. One day we were at a meeting. We were really at loggerheads. There were hard feelings between some people as to what should be done and I felt we had to break it up and I looked at them and I said, "gentlemen, we had agreed we'd break at such and such a time and we've reached that time, and I'll be glad to come back and meet with you in the morning, but I have a hairdresser's appointment and I have to go now." I could see all their faces, thinking gee that sounds just like my wife. We broke, and we came back the next morning and in probably 15 minutes, resolved the whole thing, but you know how sometimes you can just reach a stalemate. But most of the time, it was fun to have them realize suddenly that I knew what I was speaking about and started talking to me and asking me what should be done. I was able to come up with a number of very good solutions for the tax problems, not the tax problems, the tax planning, to avoid the types ofproblems.

Ms. Rogers: So how much did you charge?

Ms. Burg: I don't remember, I think maybe $35 an hour, something like that. And, of course, it was back in the late 50's so it was more than it would be today.

Ms. Rogers: But still.

Ms. Burg: Then, of course, from that I got into a lot of estate work, estate planning and then ultimately helping in the preparation of estate tax returns. In 1955, we were successful in adopting and we had a wonderful son. And everybody said, now you'll become pregnant. I would explain why physically that was impossible. That my tubes were blocked and I couldn't ovulate, I mean the eggs couldn't get down, etc. etc. and then I became pregnant. I was embarrassed to go to the doctor because he's going to think I'm crazy. I had wanted to adopt for a long time but being in an office one day and home with an infant the next day was quite a tremendous adjustment for me and in those days we couldn't really afford to have full time help. Because as I told you earlier, my "D" on what to do was being a housewife so from day one the first money I made always went into getting somebody to come in and clean the house, By that time, we had bought a small house in Riggs Park which is in northeast Washington where a number of my friends lived. I mean there was a community of young Jewish newlyweds who were there. I had problems with my pregnancy. I spent I guess 7 1/2 months really in bed and this was not very helpful with a young infant in the house. The two children are 17 months apart, so the neighbors came over and helped a lot. I never picked our son Larry up from that time until after Joan was born, when I was given permission to do so. "Mama" was someone who would lie next to him in his playpen. I was allowed to go downstairs once a day. I wore out the sofa cover lying on the sofa and his playpen was next to me so I would sing with him and play with him but never really touch him. My husband was wonderful in helping, my mother would come in several days a week and the neighbors would come in a play mah jong with me to help me pass the time and feed him if Max was delayed in getting home but it was a difficult time in my life and in a way a wonderful time. After our daughter, Joan, was born, and the doctor said I could pick Larry up, I ran into his bedroom and picked him up out of the crib and the expression on his face, I will never forget because I had never done this in months. Of course, during that time, I was not practicing. I just didn't take anything and put off whatever I had.

Ms. Rogers: So what was the break, all told?

Ms. Burg: He was born in 55 and she was born in 56. I guess by the late fifties I certainly was back in practicing part-time. I would go in twice a week to the office and my mother would come over and take care of the kids. She was wonderful with them and so I went back into practice. I guess by 58, I was back in it, and I thought I was practicing part-time and I guess about in the early 60s, I rented my own office. I rented the rear door at Fried, Frank. They had an office at Connecticut and K, and they had nobody doing tax in their Washington office. They were primarily a New York firm and there was some possible thought that I might ultimately work into the firm and do tax work from here. They had their main office entrance and then there was a rear door and so I rented the rear door where I had my name and an office and a place for my secretary and the use of their library. Don't ask me what I paid, I don't remember. It was not an exorbitant amount. This all came about because I had become quite active in B'nai Brith Women and I guess before the children were born I had remained very active in the sorority and had ultimately become international president of the sorority.

Ms. Rogers: This was the legal sorority?

Ms. Burg: No, this was not the legal sorority that I had resigned from. Phi Sigma Sigma was my undergraduate sorority and I remained very active in that. I also had become very active in B'nai Brith Women. My mentor was a woman named Irene Konigsberger whose husband had been a DC Tax Court judge and she was a remarkable woman. She was a graduate of Hunter College I guess in the early 20's. She had really wanted to, she majored in chemical engineering but couldn't go to Columbia but she took courses at Columbia and got her degree from Hunter, She had headed the synthetic rubber program at the Bureau of Standards during World War I, and then afterwards because of various things about her feelings about what was going on, she had resigned and started doing real estate and primarily worked in philanthropic activities and was a remarkable, remarkable woman. Her father came from a very interesting line of Jews in the United States. Her grandmother, I think it was, had been one of Mrs. Lee's ladies during the Civil War when the young women of the high aristocratic families were taken under her bailiwick and did volunteer hospital duties with Mrs. Lee. In a hospital in Petersburg, VA she had met a Jewish Yankee soldier who had been injured. They married and the family immediately denounced her and renounced her and they lived in New York. Irene's father had been a professor, I think of pharmacology or something. Anyway she was a remarkable woman. She became my mentor in philanthropic activities and that sort of thing and just a wonderful, wonderful person.

Ms. Rogers: And you were engaged in these philanthropic activities while you were working full time?

Ms. Burg: Well I didn't realize I was full-time because I was doing it at the weirdest hours, when the kids were asleep, and sometimes 2 o'clock in the morning, I'd go down to the office and dictate things for my secretary to transcribe when she came in because I had a full-time secretary and so I thought I was doing a part-time practice and I just never realized, you're young, you have the energy, and so I was doing it. In'64, actually in '61 my first husband underwent cardiac, aortic valve replacement. He was one of the early healthy people to do this. I say healthy in quotes, He had had rheumatic fever as a boy which was aggravated by his military service during World War II and so he was considered a disabled vet. He had surgery at Georgetown and he never fully recovered. He died in 1964. They had used a plastic valve that had gone through all sorts of testing but had not ever been in human bodies and at the time he died I think 85% of the valves had failed and in those days you didn't have a second operation. It was very early when he had surgery. So, I was widowed with an 8 year old and a 9 year old.

Ms. Rogers: I think that's probably a very good place to stop today. We've gone for two hours.

Ms. Burg: Oh really.

SECOND INTERVIEW WITH

RUTH BURG

ON NOVEMBER 5, 2005

Ms. Rogers: When we left off the last time, you said to remind you to talk about typing.

Ms. Burg: Oh right, okay. When I was in high school, I got a part-time job on Saturdays at the Department of Agriculture as a typist because I had taken typing as one of my electives in high school and worked Saturday mornings and was to become full-time in the summer after I finished school, but of course since I went on to college on a round-year basis because of World War II, I never did become a full-time typist. Interestingly, when I retired from the government, many, many, many years later, we were talking about 1943 at that point, and I retired in 1995 and saw my employment file, they had given me credit and my applications were still in there from when I had applied as a high school student for this part-time position. I did a lot of typing for my husband as he got started in his private practice as a CPA. Once I got into law school, no one knew that I knew how to type because in those days if I had, I would have ended up as a legal secretary some place, and not as an attorney. As a matter of fact, the woman who graduated the year after I did also graduated first in the class. The Dean sent her over to the Court of Claims for a position that was open. She had been a legal secretary for a major law firm and decided to go to law school and when she got to the Court of Claims she discovered it was for a position as a secretary to the chief judge, not as an attorney or law clerk and of course she turned it down. When she came back and told the Dean about it - this is the same Dean who had told me the Law School could not help me get a position when I graduated law school - he was furious at her, asked her what better could she have expected. than this wonderful job as a legal secretary to the Chief Judge of the Court of Claims. She went on to become chief attorney or general counsel of a major corporation and unfortunately died young, but that was what was happening in those days. I kept my typing ability a big secret until computers came along and then, when I was at the Armed Services Board, and became chair of the Public Contract Law Section, they could not give me any secretarial assistance to help me with working for the ABA, but there was one extra computer that had been gotten for the secretaries. The Chief Judge gave me that and I went back to typing and frankly from then on, every opinion I wrote was done on a computer. It was so much easier than writing by hand on legal paper when you had to start transposing paragraphs or inserting or deleting, and ultimately most of my colleagues also used computers with the exception of a few old-timers who could just never make the transition from yellow legal pad to a computer.

Ms. Rogers: I want to broaden that question out a little bit about the typing. I'm just wondering how you presented yourself as a woman in the early part of your career. Now we hear of women sort of having different coping mechanisms when they were the only one, or one of a very few, and I'm wondering if you can think back and sort of portray how you presented yourself.

Ms. Burg: Two ways. One way I might have already touched on. I don't recall whether I did previously. That was to play it very low key. Not to force myself on to the group for example when I was at the Tax Court, the only woman law clerk among

I guess there were 30 some attorney-advisors, if they invited me to join them for coffee, I would, if they did not, I did not say are we going today?

Ms. Rogers: Yes, you did mention that.

Ms. Burg: And ditto for lunch. So I played it low key in that regard. The other one was frankly to be one of the boys. If they told dirty jokes, you laughed, and some of them were cute, but some of them, I, you know, would not have really found that wonderful but you did not. It was hard to be, to stand out. It was very interesting as I would work with the group-- it was more interesting actually at the Armed Services Board which we will get to later. But since you asked the question, because there, since I was the first woman appointed out of 38 judges, everybody was extremely helpful. They wanted to really be my friend to help me, they were kind, they were considerate and there I could really be one of the gang. As I matured in stature at the Board, it changed. For eight years, I was the only woman until the next woman was appointed. Some of the men still remained close friends and are to this day. Others began to resent me. When I was no longer the little girl on the block who they could help and was suddenly either their equal or above them, some of them became extremely resentful and they did it in interesting ways. The comments would come back to me and, of course, the comments were always couched in terms either that I was, I remember one instance, because I was quite friendly with the Chief Judge, we'd sometimes have lunch together, as a group. I was part of the group--it was said I was "sucking up" to the Judge. Which was far from the case. I remember one time when I dissented in a case and we were in a group discussion and I said I was really surprised that I was dissenting based on a prior opinion of mine, but this was sufficiently different that I felt it should go the other way. There were some comments again that I was playing up to other members, not that I was using my own mind and ability to reason to an opinion. So that, as I matured, and as my position became a higher one, I became probably more self-confident and therefore was not quite as much the shrinking violet as probably I was when I began. You've got to remember when I started out, not only, was the fact there weren't very many women, you can't see it on your tape, but I don't know if I mentioned, I'm 5 feet tall and in those days was very thin and very petite and looked very young and people could not believe I was an attorney. I wore my hair very long and wrapped it in braids around the top of my head. I wore very heavy dark-rimmed glasses. Anything to try and look older. I remember when I was sworn in on motion in the courts of Maryland, I was just going down to the court and being sworn in and when I went in to take my oath, the woman at the desk wanted to know what I was doing there because was I cutting high school that day. (laughter) And shouldn't I be in school? I ran into lots of problems if I went into a liquor store and wanted to buy liquor. They had to see my ID. So I looked very young. People tell me I still do today. They don't realize my age, but it was that kind of thing, I had to overcome an immediate reaction on the part, especially of men, and men who were very successful businessmen, that this little girl was going to be capable of advising them about what they wanted to hear and I think I already touched on the fact that I could sense at what point in the meeting they stopped thinking of me as a little girl and began to respect the information that I was spouting to them.

Ms. Rogers: Well you just touched on appearance and I was also curious about that because one of the other things that a lot of women lawyers over the years have vacillated between is sort of looking mannish and not. There was a period in the 80's I think it was where a lot of women were wearing these little bow ties with their suits.

Ms. Burg: I never did that.

Ms. Rogers: I didn't either.

Ms. Burg: I wore suits. Of course, on the bench we wore a robe, and so it didn't matter at all what you wearing underneath. As a matter of fact, we did a lot of traveling and one time when my clothes didn't arrive, one of the judges there lent me a robe and actually it was not so huge and it did fit me and I was wearing jeans and boots underneath because I had traveled, I think was to Montana, in the middle of winter and that's how I had traveled and my luggage didn't arrive so that I could wear something a little better. I don't remember what I wore originally. I never succumbed to the fact that you had to dress like a man. I probably wore more tailored items but in the early days I couldn't afford to buy a lot of clothes. So I wore what I had. I know that I have a photo of me when I graduated law school at the awards tea and I wore a white suit, it was in May, and a very fancy big-brimmed straw hat, so it certainly could be said that I was dressed for a tea, an afternoon tea, in what a woman would wear. I wore a white suit and a large brim straw hat with, I think, flowers on it. As I became more involved professionally and reached a level where I became respected as a person, I felt it was important and always thought it was important never have to lose my femininity in order to be successful. I spoke on a number of panels where I would be the only woman at a seminar and I always made it a point to wear a bright-colored outfit rather than a dark suit. Even if I was wearing a suit, it would be in a color such as turquoise I had a red suit. I always felt it was important to not play down the fact that I was a woman and I was proud of the fact that, as a woman, I was able to reach a certain level of achievement. In my robe, of course, robes are designed for men with a tie and a collar. And then it's always been a question, I know that Sandra Day O'Connor and Ruth Ginsberg wear jabots. I always wore a scarf. I won't say always, I would wear a scarf and often a colorful scarf, or I would wear a blouse with a high-neck. Again, kind of a more colorful type of thing. Not real bright, bright. I wouldn't flout that. I tried a sort of pre-tied man's jabot and found that I didn't like it all. Since I'm somewhat large busted wearing a frilly thing didn't seem to be the appropriate thing. But I always thought it was important to maintain a certain degree of femininity.

Ms. Rogers: Well, that was very interesting. I also want to give you a chance, you had mentioned there might have been some threads you dropped at our last meeting. So I will give you a chance to sort of catch up on your early career with anything that you might have forgotten last time.

Ms. Burg: I would like to. I think I did casually mention as we were talking earlier about taking piano lessons and my mother walking us over because during the Depression you couldn't afford to ride in streetcars, etc. I continued playing the piano and studying very seriously all the way through high school. I performed a few times on the radio. I would perform at the high school and I went to what was known as the Washington College of Music. I actually received a "certificate" or degree from them worth nothing frankly, but by taking courses not only in piano but in ear training, harmony and the other courses that you would need. There was some serious consideration whether instead of applying to college, I should consider applying to Curtis in Philadelphia or to one of the school, I've forgotten the name of it. Goucher. What was the one in Baltimore?

Ms. Rogers: Peabody.

Ms. Burg: Peabody in Baltimore. I finally decided that was not for me. It was a very good decision. I did not have either the talent or the ear for doing it. Both my mother and sister have the kind of ear that they can sit down at the piano and play anything that anybody sings to them. But I was not given that gift. I had to work it out or read the music or something of that sort and so when I, I know I spoke about taking psychology tests before I went back to law school, music came out very high also and music has been a love of mine my entire life. I have not been able in the later years to play as much as I would like. Though last year, I actually started taking piano lessons again and right now have not gotten back to it after my bilateral knee replacement when I really was uncomfortable at the piano for awhile but do intend hopefully this fall to get back into again studying because I found it's the only way I can really discipline myself to sit down and play.

Ms. Rogers: Is having the lessons hanging over you?

Ms. Burg: Having the lessons, yes. Otherwise, there's always things I find that I want to do, or I have to do, or am doing, somehow get ahead of me. So that was the one thing

I had wanted to tell you because I was surprised that I had not really, I was so on the track of law, that just was, had not surfaced from my subconscious.

Ms. Rogers: Anything else you want to bring up?

Ms. Burg: I think we spent an awful long time covering a lot of stuff.

Ms. Rogers: Yeah, it was a lot. Well, where we left off as I recall was at the point where your first husband died.

Ms. Burg: That's correct. That was August, 1964, and of course, a very traumatic time of my life and the life of my two children who at that point were 8 and 9 years old which was a very difficult age for them. Any age is hard to lose a parent, but when you're young and I, you never know if you've done the right thing. I had somewhat insulated them from his illness. They knew that Daddy was someone who spent the day in the bedroom and they had to be quiet if he was sleeping or that sort of thing, but I don't think they had any idea that he was as ill as he actually was.

Ms. Rogers: Remind me what the illness was.

Ms. Burg: He had had rheumatic fever as a boy and then during his service in the Army during World War II they felt that his heart had been damaged additionally as a result. He had what was known as an aortic heart murmur but it became much worse and he lived a perfectly normal life until the 60's, played tennis, was quite the athlete and even then did not suffer any symptoms from it. But it was just the time when they felt that they could solve a person's problem by surgery and he was one of the first "healthy" people who had an aortic valve replacement, and in those days it was much more traumatic than it is today. That was in 1961, and he was fine for a while, and then in 63-64 began to show great symptoms of heart failure and it turned out that the valve had failed; As a matter of fact, when he died, I think about 85% of the valves had failed. In those days, you did not have a second operation and so he died of heart failure or cardiac failure from insufficiency at that point. An extremely traumatic time for us. He had, while he was still in a partnership, at that point, an accounting partnership, he had not been able to really work for a number of months before then or worked from the house. Luckily, he left me economically in a situation where I did not have to work, and I thought I was practicing law part time. After his death, I realized that it was not that I was practicing part time, I think I touched on this, but that I was doing it at all sorts of weird times, weird hours, go down to the office at weird hours. I still had my own office and secretary, but I was unable to get there very often at that point. When I caught myself shushing my daughter as she walked into the room as I was talking to a client, I realized she needed me much more than I needed the practice.

Ms. Rogers: That was after his death?

Ms. Burg: That was after his death.

Ms. Rogers: Had you been working up until the time of his death.

Ms. Burg: I was probably working part-time but I realized after he died, my practice was really very full-time. I was just doing it at very weird hours.

Ms. Rogers: And that was your independent practice that was in the Fried Frank office?

Ms. Burg: That's correct. So I literally closed the doors and walked out. It took me several years to wind up things that had to be done. Estates, tax returns, estates that I was working on and things of that type but I just felt that the children needed me much more than I needed the practice of law. At the time I did this, I spoke to one of the partners at Fried Frank who was the one who had been instrumental in arranging my being able to rent their rear door. This was not done casually. They weren't out looking for a tenant or something of that sort. He had kind of, he was one of the partners, and had kind of hoped that something of a more permanent nature would work out. He had been president of the PTA of our local school PTA, elementary school, had gotten to know me then, and I think I mentioned that I was extremely active in philanthropic organizations, B'nai Brith Women particularly and also in the PTA and other areas during this period of my life, and he had been an attorney at the Atomic Energy Commission. About the time that I closed my practice, Mary Bunting was appointed as one of the Atomic Energy Commissioners. She had been president ofRadcliff.

Ms. Rogers: I was just going to say was that the same person?

Ms. Burg: She was, One of her pet theses was the loss to this country of professionally-trained women who were unable or unwilling to work on a full-time basis so she persuaded the Atomic Energy Commission to run a pilot program using women on a part-time basis. Most of the women were scientists but the general counsel agreed to hire two women attorneys, and Harold Green who was the partner at Fried Frank.

Ms. Rogers: Harold Greene who became a judge?

Ms. Burg: No, Harold Green who was the prosecutor of Oppenheimer, when Oppenheimer ....

Ms. Rogers: Oh my.

Ms. Burg: … not the prosecutor, but the attorney of the Atomic Energy Commission who at the time that Oppenheimer lost his security clearance and Hal was, we never discussed politics per se, I guess we did because I think we were both those days active in the Democratic Party, but I'm not sure of that. I knew of others who were. But I'm not sure he was. And Hal, afterwards wrote a book about all this and he left the AEC. He knew the general counsel and so he told him I might be a very good candidate for one of these two part-time positions and the general counsel called me. I guess this is a good point to mention the fact that there were a number of men along the way who were very helpful and instrumental in my achieving various things. I think without the help of men who were anxious to help an individual - I don't think necessarily because they were women but some of them may be because they were women - I don't think I would have begun to achieve what I did. They did mentor us and they used their contacts which was a very important thing I think. It is today. So Hal spoke to the general counsel who interviewed me. It sounded like an ideal situation for me because I hated the thought of giving up the law and there were not that many opportunities for women part-time. This was in 1964 or 1965, I guess '65 by this time. But I was quite independent and told them I would consider a position, and would love to do it if they could find a place for me in their Bethesda office but that I would not go out to Gaithersburg because I wanted to be close enough that if I got a phone call from the school that one of the children needed me or the dog was loose again (he always loved to run up to the school and run from classroom to classroom to find them and he would scoot out the front door if someone opened the door unwittingly) that I wanted to be able to get into a car and, be within a mile of home.

Ms. Rogers: Where were you living at that time?

Ms. Burg: We lived in Bethesda but very close-in Bethesda. It was the one period in my life or one of the two periods where I moved out of the District. It turned out the then-Chairman of the Atomic Energy Board of Contract Appeals had requested one of the two positions and so Joe Hennessey, the Chief General Counsel at AEC, spoke to Paul Gantt, the chair of the Board, told him about me and I went in for an interview and we agreed that we would try it. Paul was a very interesting person. I should say I knew nothing at all about government contract law. (laughter) I did not know there was such a thing as government contract law. So I began to learn about government contract law. Paul spoke with a very heavy Austrian accent which everybody who knew him in those days and remembers to this day talks about. But he was natural-born U.S. citizen. He was born in Arizona, his parents were from Austria. At age one, his father decided he couldn't make it in the United States and they returned to Austria where he became chief of police, I believe, of Vienna.

Ms. Rogers: That would have been...

Ms. Burg: This was in, Paul must have been born in about 1910 or so.

Ms. Rogers: He'd be 95 today

Ms. Burg: No, he's dead today.

Ms. Rogers: But he would be 95 today.

Ms. Burg: It was the 1930's when the problems arose. His mother was Jewish and his father could insulate his wife but could not insulate his son from what was happening in the Nazi period. So he might have been born a little later. Anyway Paul returned. As a natural born citizen, he didn't have any trouble getting back into the United States. He returned to the United States with no money, became a paper hanger, which is a terrible thing when you think about it, and a painter. He was not at all talented in those directions. So he ultimately went to William & Mary and got his degree in law and then became quite successful working for the government and he ended up as I say chairing the Department of Interior Board of Contract Appeals and then the Atomic Energy Board of Contract Appeals. He was a marvelous mentor. He taught me a great deal and was willing to give me the leverage to do a number of things. I wrote Law Review articles with him which were marvelous to teach me the areas of government contract law. I sat in on all of the trials. There were three-panel trials, so he antagonized some of the other members of it by saying if there is a difference of opinion between a member and me, my view prevailed which didn't sit too well with some of the men there. I learned a great deal from him. I was there from 1965 until 1972. I started out working 20 hours a week and over the years, it gradually expanded in time, but I could never on paper work more than 39 1/2 hours because I was part-time. But he was wonderful about giving me compensatory time if I worked extra. It was probably not the appropriate thing to do but he did it any way. It was a great deal of flexibility because he was quite independent.

Ms. Rogers: Did you get government benefits and everything working part-time?

Ms. Burg: I got government benefits. I got leave. I got credit for it. It was somewhat different from today. It was a very specialized program. It's a shame that it hasn't been continued because I was also quite productive. So I think that Mary Bunting was right, the government benefited from this. I don't know how it would work in science if you were doing research, you can't exactly walk out. But certainly in this instance it worked out well. One regret I have is that I always meant to write Mary Bunting and thank her and it was always one of things that I meant to do and never quite got to and when I would think of it I was too busy to do it, but if I had the time, and I certainly had the time along the line, but I should have contacted her and thanked her, because I really did feel that was a major thing in my ultimate career if you want to call it a career. During that period, I met and ultimately married my present husband. He was a widower whose wife had died with children about the same age as mine. As a matter of fact, when we married, we had four children all between the ages of 10 and 12. A terrible age. And these children had an awful lot to overcome in addition to the normal problems, and I must say that they're all very close, they're marvelous siblings. We were able to cross-adopt because with deceased parents there were not some of the problems one would find if there had been parents still living. There were some problems with grandparents who didn't quite want to see this happen. But not with anything else and they are all very close today and we're a very close-knit family. I used to say we were lucky but I realize as I look back on it there was a lot of hard work that went into that. And some of what we went through was sheer hell. There's no other way of explaining.

Ms. Rogers: In the blending of the families?

Ms. Burg: In the blending of the families and the children adjusting to a new parent, a new home and all of the things that happened. We thought it was important, maybe in retrospect that was a bad decision, we felt it was important that since each of these children had had their own room in the home, that we not put them together so that they would have that degree of privacy. We couldn't afford to do it in the areas we were living in. So we moved further out into Bethesda, and that meant the ripping up and changing schools, which also was a traumatic thing for them and making new friends. Leaving the old friends behind. It was tough on them. It made life very difficult. Of course, this was in the 60s when raising children was not that easy. It's not that easy today either but this was the drug years and all of the problems that were inherent in it, and so that occupied a great deal of my time and if I had not been able to work on a part-time basis and work with someone who was very amenable to all sorts of not specific hours, it would have been much more difficult. I made it a point to not leave before the children were all off to school. I made it a point if at all possible to be there when they finished school. I spent many hours carpooling after classes so they could go to various activities and could not have done that if I had been in a different type of position.

Ms. Rogers: Did their friends' mothers work?

Ms. Burg: Very few, very few and, we didn't have a key. What do they call it now. Latchkey kids. We always had someone in the house full-time. I would not allow them to come home without someone being there. We had a wonderful, wonderful housekeeper who my husband had hired when his wife had died to take care of his children and she is with us to this day. She only works two days a week now and I really don't even need her two days a week, but she works two days for me and two days for my sister and she and her family are part of our family. We've watched her children grow up. When she married.

Ms. Rogers: You have the picture on your wall.

Ms. Burg: It's still on the wall. When she married for the third time, my husband who was half her size, she asked him to give her away and he walked her down the aisle and I was sure she was going to faint and pull him down with her. We have remained very close. They come to our family affairs, we go to their family affairs and as you said, pictures on the wall. Her youngest son graduated from Julliard and we flew up for his final recital. It's just been--it's really family. It's marvelous now, but she was part of the problem too when we married because all of a sudden she had another woman in the house. The kids are very close to her. She's got this marvelous personality and not only my children, my grandchildren. As I told you, my granddaughter spent the night with me last night and I woke her up in the morning so we could go shopping and she kind of casually opened one eye and was ready to close it again, and I said, "Lucy is here and wants to see you" and she jumped out of bed and ran and gave her a big hug. So we've been lucky in that regard. She left us for a few years to raise her own family and I remember the day we got a phone call from a woman saying she had given us as a reference - why she didn't contact us, we've never been able to figure out. The caller was looking for a reference to hire her. My husband took the call. He wasn't deaf in those days and said that if Lucy is looking for a position, we're hiring her. The woman asked whether we would recommend her and he said that he had just told "we're hiring her." He hung up the phone and called her and said, "Lucy when will you come back to work?". She came the next day. I remember that first Friday night, her husband drove the children down all dressed as if they were going to the fanciest party in the world to see us, because Friday night has always been a important family dinner for us and she wanted the family to see us. They've done very well with their children. They have five of them. Not all of them were this husband's but he adopted them and raised them all and they've achieved a lot. She said some of it's just from the association with us. And we of course have learned a lot from them. It's been a good relationship. In any event, we never had a latchkey house. But in 1972, I better pick up my professional life.

Ms. Rogers: It's all related.

Ms. Burg: Yes it is related. Because in 1971 or 1972 Paul asked me what I would want to do in the future. I said I would like, if possible, to become a judge. Of course to be appointed to one of the boards of contract appeals did not require politics. I had no political clout whatsoever. My experience had been in the courtroom and I enjoyed that. I did not enjoy some of the practice of law where you had to represent clients whose position you did not approve of. I found that very difficult and so I guess that was also one of the motivations for my leaving my practice. Some of my clients had been absolutely wonderful human beings. But some of them were not, and many of them were in real estate, because that's where tax advice were needed in the District of Columbia. My practice was a local practice and some of the builders were not the nicest people in the world. I would get a call from a client saying so and so, a subcontractor is going to call you and I told them that they had a good point and they should talk to you about it. And they'd say "don't you give that SOB one cent" and I was the bad-guy. I found that if I did not approve the position they were taking, that this was very distasteful. Now there are a lot of attorneys who can represent the client regardless of what the position is because they adhere appropriately to the rationale that everyone is entitled to representation but I found that I was not happy with that. Someone once said that I probably didn't like the gray and I wanted to put everything in the white or the black. Maybe that's true but whatever it was, I found making the decision was a lot more pleasant, pleasant is not the right term. It was something I liked more than having to represent someone whose position I felt was wrong. I would tell them it was wrong and then you'd have to go ahead and represent them, especially if you had to pay the rent. So, I thought I would really like to stay in the judicial end. Paul called the then-chairman of the Armed Services Board.

Ms. Rogers: Remind me who Paul is.

Ms. Burg: Paul Gantt was the chair of the Atomic Energy Commission Board of Contract Appeals. It was a very small board. In those days, I guess there were 11 boards. This was pre-Contract Disputes Act. of 1978, 41 U.S.C. 601-613 Many agencies that were involved in procurement, a terrible word, but government procurement and purchasing of one sort and another, had been established by delegation from the head of the agency to establish what was known as a Board of Contract

Appeals. By decisions of the Supreme Court actually, these bodies were very independent. They were quasi-judicial and that was ultimately recognized, I guess that was 1978 with the passage of the Contracts Disputes Act., supra. I'm not going into a whole history of government contract law but the Act was necessitated by a Supreme Court decision which indicated that the government did not have a right of appeal if a board deciding the dispute was the designee from the head of the agency. Therefore it was an agency decision and if you didn't like it, tough. There was a strong feeling on the part of many of us that the government should have a right of appeal if the decision was against the Government. An earlier Supreme Court decision had said if the decision was made by a board, you could not then go to the Court of Claims for a de novo trial, as had been the case until that decision. The contractor could appeal, but the government could not appeal the decision. The result of it was that these were very independent boards; a person, a member was appointed by the head of the agency. It did not require a presidential nomination. It did not require confirmation by the Senate and therefore the object was, at least at the Armed Services Board, that they looked for highly-qualified experienced people. That is true to this day because the Contracts Disputes Act requires an appointee have five years of experience in public procurement law at a high level. Now I must admit that some of the agencies don't honor this requirement exactly. The U.S. government is the largest contractor in the world and the Department of Defense is the largest government contractor so the Armed Services Board had 38 judges whereas some of the other boards had at most 3 and really didn't need 3. The dockets were such but the Armed Services Board, I probably could say, the ASBCA, although I hate acronyms, had a very large docket. The judges ran about a hundred cases each with no real clerks or secretarial help other than a pool and so, you worked very hard. Paul Gantt, the chair of the Atomic Energy Commission Board, called the then-chair of the Armed Services Board, and said that, if they had any vacancies, he had a good candidate. Now I knew the chair of the Armed Services Board. But he knew me only as Paul's assistant - legal assistant. He had no real idea about me. In any event he asked that I send over my CV and they were very impressed, interviewed me and offered me a position subject, of course, or made the recommendation that I be appointed, since it required the signature of the Army, Navy, Air Force and the Department of Defense. All of those. Not only for me. This is what was required. .

Ms. Rogers: And what year was that.

Ms. Burg: That was in 1972. Don't ask me who was president. I don't really remember. (laughter).

Ms. Rogers: Well yes you do. (laughter). Do you remember who was running that year?

Ms. Burg: Oh yes, very much so. I was campaigning but I was not at that point. Once I was appointed to the Board, I couldn't do political work. But at that point I did not. I was appointed in 72. As I say I was the first woman appointed out of 38 judges and it was an experience and a marvelous career. I have lots of stories. People say I should write some of them down. What it was like to be not only the only woman on the Board but to have high level government witnesses or private contractors suddenly came face to face with a woman. One of the first cases I ever heard was one where right after we went on, we started with the little spiel and then I went off the record for a moment, I heard this voice asking "who's that dame sitting up there?" From the expression on their faces of everyone in the room, especially of the attorney, you could tell it was the contractor who was appearing before me who asked this. The expression on his attorney's face was a sight to behold. Nobody knew how I was going to react because, of course, I was an unknown. I couldn't help it but I broke up laughing and I said "that dame is the one who is going to decide your case for you." Whereupon everyone decided to laugh. The tension was broken and we went on from there. But I had a number of interesting experiences along that line. I enjoyed it. They listened to me, the attorneys in most instances, the way my kids never did, and I was good at it.

Ms. Rogers: Now if I'm counting correctly those would have been around the years when the kids would all be going to college or in college.

Ms. Burg: I would have liked to have waited one more year. I still had one still at home in school. But frankly, when Paul said what do you want to do, I didn't think it was all going to work that fast. I figured it might take a couple of years and so did I. I did really want the Armed Services Board because that was the one that had the greatest reputation, really. And to this day does. But once it's offered to you, you don't say come back to me and talk to me two years from now. So I began. We carefully discussed it at home, and I thought we had arranged it very carefully so that I would have full-time help doing the cooking. This was the period when Lucy was not with us because she was having her own family. I had someone else and she agreed to do the cooking and all. That lasted one week. Of course, that's the way things happen. so it was a tough period. And I am sure at times I was more tense than maybe I would have liked to have been, etc. Yes it was just about the time when the kids were going off to college or in college.

Ms. Rogers: Talk a little about the subject matters that would come before you. What were the disputes? Were there things where they would pay $2000 for a toilet seat?.

Ms. Burg: Well, that's what people liked to believe. In that case the fact was very well known except that the Congress didn't want it to be known and the newspapers weren't interested in picking it up because it was not good news to explain about the toilet seat. It was not a toilet seat, it was a chemical toilet, a very sophisticated chemical toilet that could operate at very high altitudes and that sort of thing. The coffee pot was the same type of thing. Something that wouldn't explode if you got it at high altitudes. The ones that made the press because of the Christmas tree, had very good explanations. There were other instances where there was abuse of the system. As to those one of those items, even the defense contract audit agency that did the audits here had recommended that certain overhead be thrown into certain pots, rather than allocated among a number of different contracts. As to what did I do. I'd say "one day I'm an expert on paperclips and on the next day nuclear submarines." I heard and decided the largest case we ever had in those days of 75, 1975 which involved a major overrun in building of nuclear submarines, after the *Thresher* went down. Or major expenses, I shouldn't say they were overruns. It was a very complicated legal case. Whether you could have cross-contractual claims because of the situation and it was a six-month trial which at that point was the longest one we ever had. If I had not made some very tough rulings, it probably would have been gone on for three and a half years. But I did make the tough rulings, some of which the Navy has not forgiven me to this day. But none of them that were unfair to them. It was just that it made them do harder work because they had to know what the issues were instead of throwing the kitchen sink in there. The U.S. government is the largest contractor in the world. It cannot be sued as a contractor in the federal courts because of its sovereign capacity. So Abraham Lincoln established the Court of Claims for this reason. But many agencies wanted to have a final look see above the level of what is known as a contracting officer before they would let the case go on to court. So over the years Boards of Contract Appeals were established which was very similar to what the Internal Revenue Service did with the Board of Tax Appeals, which ultimately became an independent body and today is the Tax Court. There have been, there was talk over the years of possibly taking these boards out of the agencies and making them into an independent court. But frankly the cost of doing so from an administrative end would have been prohibitive to suddenly try and set this all up. It was a different time when the Tax Court was established. Each agency either has its own board or by inter-agency agreement designates another board to hear its cases. The Armed Services Board at the time I was there heard cases from 21 civilian agencies in addition to the Department of Defense. It originally started as an Army Board of Contract Appeals and an Air Force Board of Contract Appeals and a Navy Board of Contract Appeals, and right after World War II they were consolidated into the Armed Services Board. It by far is the largest Board. The reason it does a lot of the civilian agencies is because we literally sat all over the world. The U.S. Government contracts all over the world. If it enters into a contract at a military base in Germany or in Thailand or in Italy or Japan wherever it might be. I sat in all these places. In foreign countries we sat on a U.S. military base when we got there or we sat at the State Department because we would sit on U.S. territory but by contract agreement and international treaties, we were designated to decide the dispute. In the agreement it was known as the so-called disputes clause and in the event of a dispute, they agreed this would be heard, at the option of the contractor, either at the Board of Contract Appeals or at that court what is now known as the Court of Federal Claims. The decisions were final absent the a determination by the court of appeals that is was arbitrary, capricious, or a mistake in law, etc. They were appealable by either party once the Contract Disputes Act was passed to what is now the Court of Appeals for the Federal Circuit, and from there to the Supreme Court of the United States.

Ms. Rogers: So it does operate like an agency, like an administrative agency.

Ms. Burg: No. We are not subject to the Administrative Procedure Act. It operates as a non jury trial.

Ms. Rogers: The hierarchy sounds a lot like an Administrative Law Judge.

Ms. Burg: We're not.. There are 80 administrative judges created by the Contract Disputes Act, they are not part of the Administrative Law Judge group. They are not overseen by what is now OPM and that was because of the wrong wording in the statute. At the time the statute was passed, it was thought that what is now OPM would take jurisdiction over them. But they did not have the proper language in the statute. Because there were so much contention about whether the statute would go through or not, it was not shown to lots of different people to get lots of different opinions and it was pretty much engineered through the appropriate committees of Congress. It is similar but different. Many of the administrative agency decisions are not final. The head of the agency can review it and veto it. Here the head of the agency has absolutely nothing he or she say or do about it except agree to appeal it. So there is a very major distinction and that's why I say our decisions are final absent arbitrary, capricious, etc. Trials were run following many of the Federal Rules of Civil Procedure non-jury trial, which frankly is the way it should be. Some of these cases are so technical that a jury would get cross-eyed listening to some of them. Some of the stuff we heard was extreme and most of us had specialized backgrounds. It was not a requirement, but many of us had backgrounds that were of some technical nature. I had a degree in chemistry. I was a cost expert because of my background in tax law and in practicing tax law, I was considered an expert in costs and one of the major types of cases you can get if it's a cost contract, and many contracts with the federal government are cost contracts, is whether or not the costs were allowable and reasonable and, the law says allowable, allocable and reasonable, and not prohibited by any provision of law or regulation. So you would get into very highly technical accounting expert type of testimony, especially in some of your more sophisticated larger contractor cases, and where you had a contractor such as Lockheed or Boeing who have hundreds of government contracts. Questions such as how do you allocate the costs of overhead among these various bodies? And how do you allocate it between the fixed-price contracts and the cost contracts and between the civilian contracts and the government contracts. I mean the types of issues that you could face were tremendous and challenging and certainly fun if you liked to exercise your brain. And I did. They were extremely complex types of cases. Some of them were very well litigated and some of them were not litigated well at all. In some instances you would have a *pro se* contractor and then you would have the problem of how much assistance do you give to help that contractor versus figuring that they should have gotten their own attorney since it is such a sophisticated area of the law, and it really is, it's really arcane. There is really no other way of describing it. What do you do with the contractor who uses a very good attorney from Timbuktu who knows nothing about this law and wants to argue general contract law which may or may not be applicable, and has absolutely no willingness to recognize the fact there could be complex factors because of the Federal Acquisition Regulations that are incorporated into the contract. Many of these contracts, especially the Department of Defense contracts, incorporate by reference the Federal Acquisition Regulation provisions, They will specify which ones. There is a copy of the regulations sitting on my shelf over there, two red books, and this year I guess they're white, that are the Acquisition Regulations - about 4 or 5 inches of stuff. The small contractor doesn't read it. He sees that somebody wants to buy something or other, toilet seats, let's say. He has got lots of toilet seats in his inventory. He doesn't look that they have to be this dimension and this width and they have to meet these tests and he or she has to submit reports that could be pages and pages of information which requires hours and hours of work. All they see is the bottom line that gee, they can bid on this. And there are certain protections that have been set up that if the bid is so off you ask them to verify the bid, you get into a lot of litigation of this type of thing. Then you have your very sophisticated Lockheed, Boeings, and what have you that have huge staffs of attorneys working on it and they in turn, frankly, are in a position where they are making a lot of the law because like their counterpart in tax law or antitrust law or anything else are spending their hours making up how they can do it in a way that is legal and beneficial at the time.

Ms. Rogers: They are testing the limits.

Ms. Burg: Exactly.

Ms. Rogers: Okay where we were, was I asked you if all the 38 judges were based in Washington.

Ms. Burg: The answer is yes. They rode Circuit because it was much cheaper for one judge to go someplace than to bring all the people and all the witnesses, etc. except in the very large cases. Frankly, where there was a lot of money involved or a lot of complicated case issues involved, the major center for many years for attorneys who specialized in this area of law was in Washington or Dallas or Los Angeles or San Francisco. It is where you would see the majority of cases because most attorneys also like to be at home.

Ms. Rogers: Why Los Angeles and San Francisco? I guess why Dallas too?

Ms. Burg: Lots of aerospace industry. San Diego more than Los Angeles, many of the attorneys were LA law firms that opened branches in San Diego but that's where your aerospace industries were and so, this is where you went, but by far the largest number were here in Washington. I should say that our decisions were panel decisions which is not true of the Court of Federal Claims but it is one of the reasons that made our decisions so carefully thought out and valued by the people who were practicing in this area of law, because you would not have one judge deciding one way and another judge deciding another way and then saying let the appeals court take care of it. We sat independently, individually. I mean I sat by myself but then I would have a division. In my division, once my decision was written I would circulate it to members of my division. At the Armed Services Board because there were enough judges the divisions were five judges, in many of the boards it was only three judges. The chairman and vice chairman at the Armed Services Board are two of the members and then the division is composed of three other judges. So we don't go hunting for judges who were going to agree with you in the decision.

Ms. Rogers: You got who you got.

Ms. Burg: You got who you got. And it would remain that way for a number of years until there were enough retirements or changes. As there has been downsizing in the Department of Defense, I think the Board is down now to about 27 or 28 judges. But at the time I was involved with it, there were 38 and we all carried very heavy dockets.

Ms. Rogers: But explain how this works. You actually were the trier of the facts.

Ms. Burg: I would try the facts, the case would be briefed. Post hearing briefs unless for some reason they were waived but in most instance they were not waived. There were rarely prehearing briefs because you had post hearing briefs and then I as the trier of the facts, absent certain circumstances where if the judge retired or died or had such a heavy docket that it would take far too long for the decision to be issued, so it would be transferred to another judge and then the one who heard it would always be a participating member. That would happen in some instances. Because frankly some judges are more productive than others and some are more, should I say willing to go in on weekends, and evenings, and what have you, than others. But there were some who were much more productive than others. I was one of the more productive ones.

Ms. Rogers: What a surprise.

Ms. Burg: I would inherit cases. Once I had drafted a draft, it would be circulated among the members of my division and then go to the vice chairman and the chairman. Because of the load of dockets, a number of years ago the procedure of the Armed Services Board was changed and once I would write a case or a case would be written it would go directly to the vice chairman and then the chairman and if they concurred you already had a majority so it would not go to the other two. It speeded it up. On the other hand, there were some people who felt it was not, that it was better when it was all five. But that could be a very lengthy thing because the judges took this very seriously. When the decision was ultimately issued the one who would try the facts would sign the decision and the others would either concur or dissent In that respect it was more like an appellate type of decision and that is why they were carefully thought out. Because when you are dealing with four other or even two others, every word of it is scrutinized. I can tell you at the Armed Services Board this was taken very seriously. It was never one of these things, you sign mine, and I'll sign yours type of thing. And the amount of work that you would do on a case, once it was given to you to concur in it, would depend upon the complexity of a case. How much review you would do would also depend on the complexity. Sometimes you would, I can't imagine a situation where you would not at least read the briefs, so the briefs were very important, because it was up to the attorneys to call your attention to everything to make sure that the judge who had written it had covered all these issues.

Ms. Rogers: But they would accept your rendition of the facts.

Ms. Burg: Not necessarily. Sometimes, certainly if you had certain qualms with it, or if something in the brief, raised your antenna, you would go into the transcript. Every case had its own transcript so you would actually go into the transcript and read it. Now the one thing that the trier of facts generally would know, the others would not, was credibility. A transcript is not a videotaped deposition type of thing so that if credibility was involved often this would be a matter that would have to be carefully discussed with the trier of facts to say why did you feel (a) was lying and (b) was not. But there normally the trier of facts would prevail on that because you would have to rely on it. These are reputable people. There was no reason for necessarily do something other than analyzing. If you do enough of these, you begin to be able to judge some credibility, but not all. You had absolute liars on the stand who were so glib about it and they might trip themselves up and we often wondered that certain most times it was not critical, so that the extent of review that you would do would really depend on what you felt was necessary. Of course, in addition to the transcript there were exhibits. And so this case that I told you about that I tried for six months had 30,000 exhibits. So that you would give them very, very serious thought. Of course if the issue was really a legal issue or interpreting a regulation, sometimes the facts would be stipulated or you would try desperately to get the parties, often unsuccessfully, to stipulate all facts that were capable of being stipulated just to speed up the case and to avoid the problem of having to make findings on the facts that were clearly background, stipulated facts. But attorneys being attorneys would argue about whether a comma should be here or a semicolon should be there and so to get the parties to enter into a stipulation was often not as simple as one would think it should be. Decisions. How you wrote your decisions varied. The appellate court of appeals was always saying you should keep it simple but then they would reverse you if you didn't have the detailed findings in there. So you walked a fine line of trying to figure out how much you should put in. And you walked a fine line as to whether to have the findings more recitative or numbered and actually cite the transcript and exhibit per item. And if you knew that the case in all likelihood would be appealed, you would tend to take more time because of that, because you were writing not only for your own peers but you were writing for the appellate court. And the appellate court. Unfortunately once the court Reform Act was done, and they combined the Court of Patent Appeals and the Court of Claims, this was probably a very bad move because you lost the expertise on the appellate court. I knew many of the judges and as I say this was a very arcane area of law and you lost a lot of the common sense should we say that had to play into it. A very egregious example was that in order to put in a claim with the government, you had to certify the claim. But what we at the Armed Services Board had always done was if the claim was improperly certified we would stay the case, we would send it back, tell them to get a proper certification and we would then go forward with the case. The court of appeals in a decision would decide that the case was null and void from the beginning that if it was not certified by the proper party, it was nonexistent. They redefined claims to not be just, that they were entitled to X dollars but that it had been properly certified. This began 10 years of nightmares as far as many of us was concerned because the number of motions that we received. I remember speaking at a panel one time with one of the judges from the court of appeals who was somewhat annoyed by what I had to say but I gave them the actual statistics of the number of cases that we at the Armed Services Board had had of motions by the government for faulty certification and the time that it took to argue all of that and appeal it if we decided against them, etc.etc. And you never got to the merits of the case.

Ms. Rogers: And were the claimants thrown out because of statute of limitations problems because of that?

Ms. Burg: No, because there was no claim. So they had to appeal within 90 days of the denial of the claim. If there was not a claim, the six year statute of limitations could come into play. But then you could say that it was stayed by all the time and you got so much litigation on this that it was ghastly and at this particular meeting, a seminar at which I was speaking, I remember that it was up before a group of the New York Bar, one of the people in the audience -it was a very small audience because it was a breakout session of some sort - but one of the people there was the then administrator of the Office of Federal Procurement Policy and I remember him sitting up, just bolt upright, when he heard these statistics because we had been pleading for years for something to be done and within a few months the statute was passed to have it handled the way we at the Armed Services had handled it originally. That the appeal would be stayed and would be sent back for a proper certification so it wouldn't start all over again. I am kind of short circuiting some of the technicalities but that was the way it was handled. So I always said I didn't care that there was only one person in the audience as long as it was the person who could do something about the problem. I remember in a decision saying who'd have thought that 10 years after the passage of Contract Disputes Act, which was supposed to make decisions simpler and easier and faster, that we would be arguing about whether a certification was valid. We have other examples where the appellate court without really I think having a practical comprehension of what was involved becomes very, very technical or goes into some detail in a way that has created some problem. So I think that possibly merging the courts was not helpful to our area of the law.

Ms. Rogers: How was traveling, especially abroad? Did you travel as a single judge? The trier of the fact was the judge who went.

Ms. Burg: Yes.

Ms. Rogers: Tell me about traveling as a woman in this. Especially in exotic places.

Ms. Burg: Internationally, like any place else, any attorney, whether he be man or woman, knows when you are traveling on business, generally one of your first motivations is to want to get home. Because it's not fun. You go from hotel to a court room and back to a hotel. It's a very lonesome existence because we didn't travel with a law clerk. At the tax court the judge used to travel with a law clerk but here we did not. And you acted as your own clerk.

Ms. Rogers: And so, there was no staff accompanying you at all?

Ms. Burg: No staff at all. We borrowed courtrooms all over the world or all over the country and in many of the court houses, the judges were wonderful. They would be very hospitable. They would even lend you a secretary, could she help you or he help you. They would send you little notes while you were sitting on the bench, will you join us for lunch because, unlike what most people believe, most judges don't spend a lot of time at lunch time doing fun things. They will eat in a conference room ordering from the next door salad bar or sandwich bar and then you would sit and talk maybe about cases, about little things and then you would get back to work because this was a time they used for motions, signing subpoenas or similar things. I would do the same thing when I was here in Washington. It was a time that you would use to look at motions; it was a time you would use to look at disputes or things of that type that had to have subpoenas issued. We had subpoena power. You would do things of that sort. Traveling was a lonesome existence. Eating dinner at night, you don't go to the fanciest restaurants by yourself. In the early days, they sometimes were not even happy to see a woman come in by herself where a man would go in and that would be all right. I guess they figured women drank less. I don't know what it was. Now I don't think that's true any more. I think there are so many women traveling on business that hotels and restaurants have become much more acceptable of it. When we would go to the west coast, in order to save money, we would docket a group of cases, bundle them together if they were short cases and so you would generally have a week or two weeks' stint that you were supposed to go on.

Ms. Rogers: That was a long time away from home.

Ms. Burg: Yes it was lonesome.

Ms. Rogers: Did you go to any countries where women are treated very differently? Did you go to any of them?

Ms. Burg: They wouldn't let me go to Korea.

Ms. Rogers: They wouldn't let you.

Ms. Burg: No, those were the days when things were bad. I wanted to go to Korea because I had a docket in Thailand and in Japan and I could have picked up some cases in Korea and somebody else got them because they said, no we don't think it's safe for a woman to go to Korea. When I went to Thailand I was told not to issue any decision from the bench. We rarely did anyway. But if I felt inclined to, not to because if it was against the contractor, I could end up in jail. When I traveled internationally, I traveled under the cloak of the Department of Defense and I traveled with a general's rank. So if I was on a military base, I had VIP quarters and was treated very well. I remember being in Italy one time and I had this pimpled young private serving as a driver and he asked if I would like to go see the Tower of Pisa which was on our way to the airport. He said, "I've never had a person with as high as rank as you in my car before." So they obviously didn't give me the top person to drive me. I had some interesting experiences traveling as a woman. I remember staying in a hotel in Portland, Oregon, the biggest hotel in town. I've forgotten the name of it now. Of course, I would always ask for a government room because we were on government rates and even though I stayed at hotels like this because I did not want, I was careful not to stay at second or third-class hotels frankly. It always cost me money regardless. You never cover your costs and hotels with per diem even if you've got a government room and you're always in the smallest room in the hotel. In this hotel in Portland I was all the way down in the corner and I was in the room one night and there was a knock on the door and I said "who is it", and someone said "it's me, honey." I said, what! He said, "so and so down the street told me you were doing business tonight in this room, so let me in." I said "you have the wrong room." I didn't open the door but I yelled you have the wrong room. He said that this is the room they told me to go to. And I said "you have the wrong room". He said "aw come on honey, stop giving me such a tough time and let me in." I said "I am a federal judge. If you don't leave this instant, I am calling down to the desk and telling them that someone is trying to break into my room" and that ended it. I think that was the most difficult one I ever had. On the whole, especially as the years went by, and people got more used to seeing women travel by themselves, it was more that it was a lonesome existence. You had work with you so you would do your work, you had books with you, but what people don't realize when you are sitting on a case, is the amount of that case that you take home with you at night and think about. it. They just think that the judge just reads, forgets everything, and makes them do all the work of preparing the witnesses and shows up the next morning, and says let's continue. But that's not the case. If you're a responsible judge and I like to think that I was and I'm told that I was, you take a lot of it home with you. Sometimes it's the fact that you learn early on in the trial case that you are not dealing with a jury. You don't have to prove that you know everything. At the beginning, you feel that you have to have fast answers to everything. But I think as you mature, become more secure in what you're doing, yes you give fast answers, if there are objections and things of that type, but if a valid question is raised, and you feel you've got to think about it, you tell the parties, "I'm going to consider this and rule later." Especially if it doesn't impact on the particular witness or the witness is going to be carried over. Later might be an hour later and you will go do some research or it might be over lunch while you think about it but it might be overnight while you are thinking about it and you are giving it careful consideration. So you take a lot of it home with you. You might want to go over your notes just to make sure you haven't missed anything. One of the things that we could do, since it was a non-jury trial and I used, was my prerogative of asking questions. I made sure I got in the record what was necessary. I think one of the worst things that can happen to a trial attorney or any attorney is to have what I call an unknown expert. I would use my expertise to make sure that the proper questions were in that record. Not to use it to decide a case. I would do this is was several ways. One would be that I would use my prerogative to ask questions. But on the other hand I also had learned--I told you Paul Gantt who was my teacher. I had learned a number of things from him and one of the things I had learned, which was a terrible habit that he had, is that he would interrupt an attorney questioning a witness and maybe take anywhere from two minutes to an hour or longer questioning that witness and then would tell the attorney to pick up where he or she left off. Sometimes when the attorney would resume the questioning, Paul would say "we've covered that material already and move on." I felt that this was very unfair to the trial attorney. So the practice that I developed was that I would jot down notes as we would go along with questions that I wanted answered. Often, they would be covered but in another order. The attorneys would have their own way of presenting the case but after direct and cross-examination, if those matters had not been covered, I would use my prerogative and ask the questions, and then I'd explain to the parties and counsel that this was what I was doing and then I would say "I'll afford you any opportunity that you might want to examine on the areas that I am raising" because technically it's not direct or cross. So that meant I had those notes to review at night because as the questions would be asked, I would strike these off but I would want to make sure that everything I felt was important was covered. As I said, these cases were extremely technical.

Ms. Rogers: Are these cases used as precedents for other cases?

Ms. Burg: Yes. That is the where the value of the panel decisions came in. They became precedent. Not by another board but by our board.

Ms. Rogers: In terms of precedents, did you ever decide a case in a particular way that everybody signed off on and it was later taken in a direction that you hadn't anticipated and that you didn't like.

Ms. Burg: Oh yes. I was often shocked when cases that I had written were cited in a brief, because attorneys always want to cite the cases of the Judge they go before, and they would cite some things that I had never said or never thought I had said. I would go back and read the case and sure enough in many instances, I had not said it. One of the things I used to urge attorneys to do, was to read the cases before they cited them and not just the headnotes. Because often headnotes or abstracts didn't have a lot to do or might not have completely gotten the idea. Yes, they might go in a direction you didn't mean. The judge I clerked with at the tax court was marvelous in training me to look at a case if at all possible and saying now, is this too broad, might it be interpreted in a way beyond what we intend it to be. You don't always catch it. So sometimes you would do it and sometimes you would be compelled in a later decision to say the parties have misunderstood the import of what we were saying and that it should be, that goes far beyond what it was meant to be. There were instances where we were reversed by the appeals court and that you would either say "while we don't agree with this and our precedents are to the contrary, we are bound by what the appellate court has said." Or there were some times when you would feel compelled to reverse it. Or where you would have another panel who felt it should go differently and you would have to reconcile them either by reversing or by narrowing or by qualifying what had been said. But you would not ignore them.

Ms. Rogers: Did you ever make a decision that you actually look back and thought you wrongly decided?

Ms. Burg: An interesting point. I can't say I ever did. I might have made a decision that I would have liked to have gone the other way but felt that either the law or the facts made it impossible for it to be done. I recently heard another judge say, the appellate court, you might not always think its right but they have the last word. Of course, there is one famous case in our field where I felt that the panel was absolutely wrong and wrote a very strong dissent. I was the trier of that case and I dissented and in very nice, ladylike, strong language. The appellate court agreed with me, so for once the appellate court was right. They practically adopted what I had had to say in my dissent. I can't say that I ever felt that I decided a case wrong. I might have felt that had the facts been presented properly the case might have gone the other way or I might have decided it differently. Lots of our cases were factual decisions.

Ms. Rogers: Have you ever been on jury duty?

Ms. Burg: I've been knocked out of the box as the first person every time I was called. I would have loved to have been on jury duty.

Ms. Rogers: I was once and what you just said reminded me of that.

Ms. Burg: I was called a number of times and I guess if I always ended up in the jury box, I was the always first *voir dire* that was out of there. Even though the judge would say to me while questioning me, "do you feel that this would impact at all on your ability to serve as a juror." And I'd say "absolutely not." I didn't think it would. But I'm sure they felt I might be too persuasive. No I know judges who have served.

Ms. Rogers: In this town.

Ms. Burg: No, I've never served. But I ....

Ms. Rogers: So they didn't catch you even before you were a judge.

Ms. Burg: No, they didn't catch me before I was a judge. In those days, they were trying to get rid of most lawyers on the juries, too. Now I think the jury pool has changed. That is, that essentially, I guess is my Board experience. I sat on the Board for 22 years. I became one of the more senior judges, I mentored a lot of young people who are very complimentary. I have always found mentoring very important.

Ms. Rogers: When you left, how many women were there on the bench?

Ms. Burg: 8.

Ms. Rogers: 8 out of?

Ms. Burg: I guess at the point 30, I guess there were about 35 at that point. Now, I guess the number of women is down to 6. A lot have retired and have not been replaced. That's not true, one was replaced. Finally, they merged the NASA board and the Corps of Engineers board so the 28 is not really a valid number in terms of 38. Two of the smaller boards that never should have existed became part of our board. But, over the years, as I became more senior, I had a very good reputation among the private bar, not as good a reputation among the government bar. Many felt I was "biased" for the private bar but essentially what it was and I don't think I was, because the majority of my decisions were in favor of the government actually. Many of the members of the government bar had never served in the private sector. I know some government attorneys who have then made the transition to the private sector and their whole attitude has changed. One of whom was very instrumental in getting some terrible statutory provisions in what is known as the Truth in Negotiation Act, 10 U.S.C.2306a and 1 U.S.C. 254A, and then when he went into private practice, realized the mess he had made of it. They just do not understand. By the same token, a lot of people in the private sector do not understand what it's like to be in the government and the responsibility that you feel for the government fisc and the responsibility that you feel for being more careful. You know, if the color of the paint on the wall of your house is not exactly maybe the one you selected but it's close enough but you will accept it. But if you're inspecting it for the government and it is to be this shade and it's not, it's your job to refuse to accept it. That's your obligation. And so, I think it would be helpful if people served both sides and had the experience.

Ms. Rogers: Like Take Your Daughter to Work Day.

Ms. Burg: Exactly, exactly. So I think from that aspect I enjoyed what I was doing. I think I paid a price for what I did in terms of raising my children and working part-time. Because I was interviewed for the then Court of Claims.

Ms. Rogers: That was going to be my next question. If you had ever wanted to be on one of the other courts?

Ms. Burg: I was interviewed for the Court of Claims in the Carter administration. It was the first judicial panel to be empowered, to be put in. He certainly was looking for women. There had never been a woman on the Court of Claims and there were a lot of people who felt that I would get the appointment. I was one of the 23 final group interviewed by the panel, The Court of Claims dealt with government contracts as one of its subject matters but also did tax cases. I had the tax background also. And then ultimately when the Court of Appeals for the Federal Circuit was set up, I had not only that, but I had some patent law experience because I had a degree in chemistry and had very early on done some patent law work for a patent attorney. That was before I really got going in my own practice so that I had three of the areas of expertise, but I didn't have any political clout. When I was interviewed or in 1978, when Carter first came in, when I was interviewed for the Court of Appeals, rather for the Court of Claims, I did not have any political clout and I was very naïve in that regard. Also the group that interviewed us, some of them had a comprehension of what we did, but a lot of them did not. The list that went over to the White House was 5 white males. Carter rejected it. The second list was 5 white males, and he appointed 2 who were very good and served as very good judges. One of them is still serving as a senior judge for the Court of Appeals for the Federal Circuit. They were very good but they had lots of backing. One, I believe, had been the deputy Solicitor General, and they had lots of political clout. I had been naïve enough to think that politics would be involved when it got to the White House but not that it would happen within the selection committee. Years later talking to a member of the group, I learned that what is done is you vote for my guy, I'll vote for yours type of thing. But I was very naïve. There was never another vacancy there during the Carter administration. By that time I became very active in the Public Contract Law Section of the American Bar Association, not because of that, but just because I felt if I was going to pay my dues, I either had to be active or I should forget it. Ultimately I went on to become chair of the Section. Again the first woman who ever chaired it and that was an interesting story because some of the men as I was going up the line tried to bump me. I was convinced they were doing it because I was a woman. They had all sorts of reasons, none of which made any sense and like maybe if a Board judge should not be chair whereas one of the first chairs of the section had been the chairman of the Board and a good friend of theirs, whom as a matter of fact, they were pushing for the Court of Claims spot that I was also being interviewed for. He didn't get it either. Even with his political clout. But I never had another chance. There was no vacancy during the Carter administration. Frankly when the Republicans came in, I didn't have the proverbial chance of a snowball. Because all they would have to do is ask the organizations to which I contributed like the Wilderness Society or the American Civil Liberties Union membership and that sort of thing and I could forget it. I had become emotionally involved with the Court of Claims matter and it took a toll and I never allowed myself to become emotionally involved again. I was interviewed several times for a District Court position but was never given one, they never offered one. I had a serious question in my mind whether I really would like a District Court appointment because of the criminal law cases.

Ms. Rogers: By that time, you didn't know how to work it politically or were you still sort of hands off.

Ms. Burg: I was still kind of . . . . You know, once I was where I was, I had to stay hands-off. I think I spoke to, who's the one who got the Margaret Brent Award this year, Judy Lichtman, early on but she felt there was not much she could do. I guess that might have been for the Court of Claims one. It might not have been. I would have . . . Without seeking it, I was recommended for a trial judge position at the Court of Claims early on and that would have been a position I would have liked. I was literally at the top of the list for many years and I was never offered the position. They never had a woman and the day I was interviewed by the judicial selection committee for the appointment to the Court of Claims, a woman who was a member of our board at the time but was at the bottom of the list because of other reasons, very bright but took forever to get decisions out, was appointed as a trial judge at the Court of Claims. I think she really had problems. None of us could ever understand what the problems were. She had serious problems, became a real recluse. She had clerked for one of the judges of the Court of Claims and so she was appointed as a trial judge and went over there, I'm convinced she was appointed so they could say they at least had a woman who was a trial judge on the court. I was told once by someone, and whether this is true or not I've never been able to find out, but one of the former chief judges of the Court of Claims had said as long as he had anything to do with it, "that Jew girl will never get an appointment". Trial judges were named by the judges. Whether this is true or not, I don't know. I really don't.

Ms. Rogers: Well, that's remarkable. And that was in the 70's?

Ms. Burg: It was in the 70's. It might have been he didn't like me as an individual and just used the term. I just don't know. I do know that, of course, once the Court Reform Act came along and they merged the courts they didn't appoint any more trial judges. If they had I would have become a judge at the court at what is now the Court of Federal Claims and I know a number of them over there. I knew the

Chief Judge of the Court of Federal Claims, both of them, the two first ones, I knew fairly well. I was on panels with them. I'm on the advisory board of that Court now. So I think I would have liked that one only because, and of course, in those days you didn't need a Senate confirmation, but if you were sitting there as a trial judge when Court of Federal Claims came along, you were automatically merged in and then some were subsequently reconfirmed and because it is a 15-year term and I suspect that if I had been on there, I don't mean to be egotistical, but I think I would done a good enough job that I would have been reconfirmed because the reconfirmation there really is not a real political thing. To be appointed there now is a very political thing. I mean to be appointed there now is very political. Mary Ellen Coster Williams, a Democrat, was appointed as a pairing off against a very conservative Republican this term. But I never really spent the time getting all the political clout that I might have needed. I don't know. It's an academic question. So you never really know. But that one I would have liked. The District Court position I am not sure I would have liked.

Ms. Rogers: It would have been very different for you.

Ms. Burg: It would have been very different from what I did and I do not know whether I would have enjoyed it as much. I think by that time I was secure enough in what I was doing and enjoying it enough. To be there at the Court of Appeals I don't think I would have liked it as much as the trial work. I enjoyed the trial work. It was a challenge. It was a challenge dealing with the witnesses, with the attorneys, having the questions, etc., so I enjoyed all of that. I never minded working hard and I think that is why I would have made a good record as a trial judge at the

Court of Federal Claims and I think they, as people say, they needed me more than I needed them, because there had been some bad decisions.

Ms. Rogers: Well, we've been going a long time. So I think we should probably wrap up, but do you have anything that you want to wrap up with today?

Ms. Burg: This has been an interesting experience and I (laughter) many years. And more to go. I think we've covered a great many of my years at this point.

Ms. Rogers: Well, yeah, but we have to talk about your retirement, we have to talk about your retirement, so called. We have to talk about other sort of observations over the long haul. I've been jotting down things that are yet to be covered. So the question is if there is anything that you now caught that you...

Ms. Burg: No, I have not thought of anything.

Ms. Rogers: You'll think about it tonight.

Ms. Burg: I'll think about it tonight. One of the things I know and that's why I probably would have had a terrible time going through a Senate confirmation. I'm not a fast responder. I don't answer quickly, off the cuff. My ....

Ms. Rogers: You're stream of consciousness.

Ms. Burg: My years of doing what I have done have given me the opportunity in what I was doing to think about things before I quickly respond. That's not true, because I was certainly very fast in making rulings, you know if I had objections on evidence and that sort of thing. I had no problem making them. I had no problem making decisions. I guess one of the things, and we might go into that later is, what are some of the characteristics of being a good judge. I worked with trying to devise questions that you could ask a potential candidate, and we found the two most difficult questions one could ask in many ways were the ability of a judge to decide the case and the temperament of the judge once they got on the bench. Because a person may become over-imbued with power and become a very, very nasty, nasty person on the bench. Attorneys are used to, when they are dealing with the clients, saying they can either decide, you know you've got a 2 percent chance of winning or a 98 percent chance of winning, or a 99 and 44/100 percent, but there is always that little out and when you are a judge, you can't do that. You've got to decide the case. And we found that people who were appointed and were marvelous attorneys and marvelous people, but either hated to have to make the decision or fretted about it so long that it took forever to get a decision out of them because they just didn't know how. They were unwilling to bite the bullet and make the decision. You asked earlier if there was any time I made decisions that I would have taken back later on. I can't think of any, I will have to go through and think about that question. That's why I hesitated when you asked me. I can't imagine that there weren't. At the time you make them you're doing the best that you can. Certainly there were some instances where I was reversed, there were some instances where I dissented and possibly I was wrong. But I was doing my honest best to make the best decision at the time.

Ms. Rogers: This is a good place to stop.

3rd INTERVIEW WITH RUTH BURG

SATURDAY, DECEMBER 17, 2005

Ms. Rogers: I went back and looked at where we left off and you were still working when we left off. We haven't even gotten to your so-called retirement yet. But let me start by asking you a sort of broader question that I've been meaning to ask, which is when you think about through the path your career has taken and when you started it. Do you have any thoughts about if you were starting to be a lawyer now or even 10 or 20 years ago if it would have been different for you, if you would have chosen different things, or pursued other interests, or maybe not even been a lawyer at all?

Ms. Burg: Well, as we discussed before, I started out being a doctor and in all likelihood had I not met my first husband, I would have either finished medical school because I'm not a quitter or I have would have done gone some place outside of Washington and done a graduate degree in physiology or biochemistry. Having said that, I think that I was much better off going into law. Would I have done things differently? Yes, I probably would have because life shapes what you do. I went into tax both because of my interest in math and because my husband was an accountant, a CPA. I probably, of course, would have stayed in tax, but I possibly would have been able to retain some political connections and I think would have ended up trying to get into the judiciary. But probably would have been in a better position to have gotten an Article 3 appointment. I was interviewed for one District Court position, but I really wasn't interested in it. I used it as an experience exercise because, having been interviewed for the Court of Claims which was when Carter first came in and feeling that I made a terrible mess of the interview, I had no coaching, no assistance before I went in there. I really felt that I could have done much, much better and so I kind of used this as an experience thinking it might help me, but of course no other openings ever opened up in the Court of Claims when a Democrat was in office, very frankly, and the chance of getting a Republican.

Ms. Rogers: That's exactly where we left off the last time. We were talking about that.

Ms. Burg: I like the Judiciary. Somebody and I might have said this earlier said I don't like things that are gray so I try to put them to the black or into the white and maybe that's true into little pigeonholes. I like the making of decisions even though they were difficult at times and I liked the challenge of it and as I used to say, sometimes the attorneys listened to me a lot more than my children ever did. Maybe it was a sense of power, but I don't think I used it adversely, I don't think I was overcome as unfortunately some people are when they take the bench of being so imbued with the power that they become really very nasty individuals. I don't think I would have done differently in terms of devoting my time to my children, even though it impacted on my profession. If there had been other ways of doing it in all likelihood, but my family always came first and if that meant that I didn't achieve certain things that I would have like to have achieved, I was willing to make that compromise. Does that answer your question?

Ms. Rogers: Yes, it's a start. (laughter) Another issue we sort of left with was what do you think the characteristics of a good judge are and how that suited you?

Ms. Burg: A good listener, the ability to understand and grasp quickly the issues that are presented to you, the willingness to make decisions without taking an interminable period of time. That's not to say that there isn't some time before you come up with them, but some of them you have to make pretty quickly. You have objections about evidence or something of that sort. You can't just rule on some of them. Some of them you could defer. After I became more experienced that I didn't have to prove that I knew what I was doing, I had no compunction about saying I will take this under advisement if it did not impact and then give them an answer maybe an hour later, maybe a day later, but if you have a witness on the stand and you know it's the one opportunity you have, you have to be able to, the ability to control to a certain extent, the willingness to be wrong, be reversed, or sometimes even if you are reversed, you say, they may not be right, but they have the last word, and not to take it personally. The ability to reason through and that's where I think my science helped me. Reason through a set of facts to a result. I've had debates with my husband, who is a scientist, because, of course, he feels things must be absolute in terms of results and law is never absolute in terms of results. So I think in that respect, I think that those are the essential characteristics.

Ms. Rogers: Do you think that women and men are any differently suited to this?

Ms. Burg: I think women bring a different view to the law, not only to being a judge but to the law itself. Maybe it's because of the maternal instinct. I think they look at things a little differently. I'm not talking about legislating the law. Activism on the bench is something that's very popular right now and I think it's a lot of words. You're a judicial activist if the other side doesn't like your results--is what it essentially boils down to. But I think that a certain amount of humanity, of recognition of what the world is all about has to go into making your decisions. It does have an impact. People who says that a judge decides things based on the record is correct, but building that record, whether you want to recognize it or not, is who you are, and I think that has very major impact. The problem coming up with what is right or wrong with how you would approach it and many of the cases before you are very tight difficult cases and whether you want to recognize it or not, what you are is going to have something built into it. I think women can be much more compassionate. That's a terrible word to use in this administration.

Ms. Rogers: No. It's a fine word. You can't let them steal the word.

Ms. Burg: I think that a recognition of what the world is all about is built into many of the cases.

Ms. Rogers: Do you think that women have more of that practical sense?

Ms. Burg: Maybe it's a practical sense, maybe it is more of being willing to understand the emotions of the individuals who are involved and how that impacts on the disputes before you and things of that sort.

Ms. Rogers: I mean a lot of the recent studies of sort of gender roles have been to the effect that women really like to build agreement and consensus, and men like winners and losers a lot more. I don't know if that has anything to do with the functions of a judge.

Ms. Burg: That's an interesting way of putting it, but I'm not sure. I'd have to think about that. I think maybe because I know a number of women who are very good negotiators, get a lot of settlements even when they're on the bench. But I know a number of men who do that also. And I know a number of women and men who are not interested in doing that. And so I don't know whether you can make that kind of a generalization or not. It all boils down to who you are and what you are and what you believe in. Back to your earlier question, I might have gone more into another area of the law you know as I think about it. Maybe the area that you're in actually. I am very interested in the world, having spent in my younger days when I had the time or a lot of time doing work with various philanthropic organizations. Those were the things that interested me, provoked me, and made me want to do something about them, and it was a time in the world when that was going on. It still is but I mean this was when people began to be more concerned. The other night I was with a group of scientists. The wife of one of the other scientists there and she and I sat at the end and talked. She is in the process of writing a book. She's 58 years old. A social worker, a writer, and she is writing a book on Eleanor Roosevelt and started it out with the correspondence between Eleanor Roosevelt and J. Edgar Hoover, of which there is a great deal.

Ms. Rogers: I didn't know that. That's fascinating.

Ms. Burg: She found that didn't lend itself to enough of a book so it has gone more into development of what has happened with civil liberties starting with that and where it has gone on or what is happening. I was unaware she said that some effort has been made to stop calling it the J. Edgar Hooverbuilding.

Ms. Rogers: There have been very many calls for that. Richard Cohen of the *Post* has written many columns about it.

Ms. Burg: So we got discussing where civil liberties is today and looking at it as more of a social issue. You should look at the new book. It will be a fascinating book. The other book she wrote I have sitting over there. She has done several. The last published book is the correspondence of Eleanor Roosevelt. The whole book is really primarily letters written to or written by Eleanor Roosevelt. She was given access to a great deal of the library up at Hyde Park in New York. As she said Hoover would write one thing and he would turn around and do another.

Ms. Rogers: Well, when you say that might have been an area you would have pursued. When you were sort of beginning your career, what were lawyers doing in terms of, I'm thinking of what organizations they might have been in. I guess the NAACP Legal Defense Fund was active.

Ms. Burg: That was one. The Anti-Defamation League of course was very much involved and I was active in Jewish organizations, you know. In our temple, I was on the board, and my first husband was an officer of the congregation.

Ms. Rogers: But were there lawyers at ADL at that time? There are now. I just don't know if they were pursuing litigation at all.

Ms. Burg: You know it's hard to remember, I'm sorry to say. Yes, I'm sure, certain there were. If not, professionally, certainly many of the volunteers. They were mostly men. There were a number of lawyers in the organization . In those days B'nai Brith Women was part of B'nai Brith. They split off in subsequent years. The women wanted to get a tax exemption as a 501(c)(3) organization, and the men said it couldn't be done. Under their organization, the way B'nai Brith had 501(c)(3)s was to create separate groups under the umbrella but they were separate from the organization itself. I went in and got a 501(c)(3) exemption for the women, which the men said couldn't be done. We did it. Certainly there were a number of women involved at that point. Hillel was another group that did have 501(c)(3) and you did have a lot of attorneys involved in that one. I think you had as much. Then they were very active in the NAACP and then the Civil Rights Movement in that day and a number of the women whom I knew were very very active. One who was the international president ultimately of the B'nai Brith Women, was also very active in the NAACP. There were meetings. I remember a meeting over at Catholic University in which I participated along with a number of other women. This was the group who took the leadership in desegregation. That was where everything was focused in those days.

Ms. Rogers: Right. There wouldn't have been much activity in the women's movement at all.

Ms. Burg: No, no. As a matter of fact, I think I discussed some of that with you very early on that women were supposed to know their place.

Ms. Rogers: Very different times.

Ms. Burg: It was.

Ms. Rogers: You mentioned last time that you thought, or think, that mentoring has been very important and I was curious whether you had any protégés over the years who were young women that you take particular pride in.

Ms. Burg: Oh yes, there are several of them who are still quite active. One in the last two years was sworn in as a judge on the Court of Federal Claims. In her investiture speech she was very generous in thanking me and mentioning me and my mentoring, That is Mary Ellen Coster Williams.

Ms. Rogers: I have heard that name. And how had she been connected to you. Did she clerk for you?

Ms. Burg: No, we didn't have individual clerks. Actually, she was very active in the Young Women Lawyers Section, of the Young Lawyers Section of the American Bar Association. She was on the council, our council, as the representative from the Young Lawyers. I met her that way and then she got interested in our field of the law and over the years became quite active in it and then she ultimately was a member, an administrative judge in the GSA Board of Contract Appeals. Carol Park-Conroy who is an Administrative Judge at the Armed Services Board is another one who I am very proud to see how she has become an outstanding judge. She was a good trial lawyer at the Department of Justice when she came over. So it was not as if she was a novice. Some of our law clerks have gone on into other positions, and we had some women law clerks, but not many because there were not that many who were really interested in getting into our area of law. It's a very arcane type of law. I can't claim all the credit for their achievement but Karen Hastie Williams over at Crowell & Moring, Marcia Madsen is now with Mayer, Brown. These are women I spent time with. I won't say I took them under my wing but maybe I did. There are a few women I still see and are friendly with. Our time is so limited. I don't have that much time with them. I guess those are the ones who come to mind directly. I don't remember whether I talked about the Gang of Five. At the American Bar Association annual meeting, in the early days there were five women involved with our Section. Over the years, we would always get together for lunch and a meeting and we got out. As more women began to become active in our field which was Public Contract Law section of the ABA, we would have people, more women join in and we started having a more formal type of lunch, not really formal, but somebody would take it upon herself to organize it a little more.

Ms. Rogers: The women's caucus of the section.

Ms. Burg: I guess that would be a way of talking about it and it kind of grew and I used to tease some of the women. We would go into the ladies room and they'd be complaining about the line and I'd tell them about how glad I was to see it because I remember the days when I was the only woman in there. Two or three years ago when the American Bar had their meeting here in Washington, we had a luncheon and when I walked into the room, I literally broke into tears because there were 120 women there, which was a lot different from days when I had started attending.. Then two years ago, the section honored me by making the luncheon a formal activity of the section during the annual meeting. They now have the luncheon to which men are also invited and it's been named after me. It is the Ruth Burg Luncheon. I was really very honored and shocked and I don't know if you can see it, I'll show it to you ....

Ms. Rogers: You've got to turn, I can't hear you. You don't if I can see it but,

Ms. Burg: You can't see it, but there is a crystal piece over there which they presented to me at that time. Actually it was when Mary Ellen Coster Williams was the chair of the section. I was very moved.

Ms. Rogers: I guess you've seen over the years that the ABA generally has gotten a lot more women-centric.

Ms. Burg: Oh, yes. Well I think that the Women's Commission has had a lot to do with that and I think also time has helped. I think that the whole recognition of women as lawyers in the field as women have also matured. I remember a young woman who applied for one of our judgeships and her application. She had no experience. She was 26 years old and said she should get it because she was a woman. Of course I think that does a disservice in women in the law, to women in any area. I think you have to earn it, and I think time has helped as you see more women in the law schools, I am hopeful that you will also see more women on the bench as time goes on because they become more experienced and become better respected. It has improved both because of the efforts that have been made but also I think time has helped.

Ms. Rogers: What did you think-- this was a very interesting segway into something I was thinking of asking you the last time I think. What did you think of that whole Harriet Miers Supreme Court nomination? The entire trajectory of it and you know how much it impacted women.

Ms. Burg: I think she deserves a tremendous amount of credit for what she achieved. Knowing a number of Texas attorneys -- men -- that she achieved, what she achieved in terms of being President of the State Bar and being chair of the law firm, speaks very highly for her and she deserves tremendous amount of credit. I think as far as being nominated for the Supreme Court, I had grave concerns about her lack of constitutional experience. You can argue some of the men who were appointed there, were nominated without experience, don't have it either and I think they deserve as much scrutiny. I think on the Supreme Court you need people who are good scholars in Constitutional law and I don't know that she had that. I don't think that the Supreme Court is a place for on-the-job training. So I had grave concerns about it. As far as whether she was dropped because she was a woman, I don't think the conservatives were looking at her as a woman. I think they were looking at it as if she was someone who was going to try and overturn *Roe v. Wade* and there would, I don't think the fact that she was a woman that was a matter of concern to them as much as that she might not share their views of right to life.

Ms. Rogers: How about the press treatment of this whole chain of events and whether the female angle had any impact on that?

Ms. Burg: Interesting question. Just to the extent that *Roe v. Wade* is a female issue, one could argue or say that that was the way this was treated. I'm not sure that the big concern that I had was much with *Roe v. Wade* as just the general Constitutional thing, and that was not something that was focused on a great deal by the press. There they did focus more on the women issue, which is a very serious issue. You wouldn't have thought that people would go back to the days of illegal coat hanger abortions, I think to some extent, I criticize the women's movement for allowing for it to become a question of abortion versus choice. I'm not sure the women are the ones who are to blame for that as much as that may be framed as the issue by a man.

Ms. Rogers: Tell me a little more about what you mean by that.

Ms. Burg: I had 14 miscarriages. I desperately wanted a child. I can't say that they knew that every one of them was, but there were certainly some of them where it was never a question. How do I feel about abortion if I were to become pregnant? I don't know, I never had to face that issue. But I think it's a decision that I should have been able to make, no court should make it for me. That's why I'm talking about it as being a question of choice. I think it's a private matter. I don't think this is a matter that the court should step into. The old saw, if men bore children, abortion would be legal is certainly apt.

Ms. Rogers: I think the quote is "abortion would be a sacrament."

Ms. Burg: I remember an argument I had with one of my colleagues one day at lunch. It was wrong. I shouldn't have had the argument with him there. It became a shouting match on my end. He's a devout Catholic. People thought we would never to speak to each other again. We did. I mean we respected each other as individuals. I did not respect his views on that. I still don't. I think he is absolutely wrong, but again I think that that's what I mean when I say I think it is really a matter of individual choice whether you want an abortion or not. Do I believe in abortion, of course, in the right place at the right time, and the right person. I mean if someone decides that is what they want, that's their right. I don't think it's up to anybody else to impose their position on me.

Ms. Rogers: What do you think about the fact that it seems to be now the centerpiece of every court proceeding. Every court nomination battle.

Ms. Burg: Well, that I think is terrible. And I don't know how one can avoid it. As I say my concerns for Harriet Miers was not necessarily where she would come down on abortion. That was absurd. I'm not sure that is the kind of thing that we can.... I have very mixed feelings whether this should be the lynchpin for whether or not a person should be confirmed or not. I think it was a big mistake-- I call it a mistake-- to elect the president we have because it was evident that this was going to be the kind of person he would nominate for judicial positions. I said it at the time in talking to people. "Do you realize that if you vote for Bush this is what's going to happen?" and they either didn't care or didn't realize the import of what this would mean. Because what you're doing is creating a situation for many years to come. I think this country can withstand four or eight years. You might not like it but you can withstand it, but to change the whole tenure of the bench. I don't think it's a question of judicial activism. It gets back to what I said. I think you bring to your decisions your whole background, how you are going to interpret various things. So what do I think about it? I think it's deplorable, but that's where it has come. Not because that people shouldn't focus on it, because this is where this country has kind of been forced to focus. I don't know who is to blame. The ultra-conservative party? I think you can say it's not the religious view as much because certainly there are a lot of Catholics even who have been willing to stand up and say they are pro-choice despite the impact. In this country at least, - and I'm talking about politicians – it's become "Let's make it the litmus test for every judge who is appointed." I find it a very sad, sad situation and there's not a lot we can do about it until we get to the next election, and then whether that will change it, I don't really know because I think, it's been said there and I think it will take a long time for us to get away from it.

Ms. Rogers: Could you have foreseen that *Brown v. Board of Education*, 347 U.S. 483 (1954), on the desegregation decisions would be so settled and institutionalized?

Ms. Burg: Are they? I think they are.

Ms. Rogers: I haven't seen confirmation hearings that are centered around whether you agree with equal accommodations or not.

Ms. Burg: That's true. To that extent, it is a settled issue. But as a practical thing. Do we really have desegregation in the schools? I'm not sure.

Ms. Rogers: Now the schools have been very difficult. I think that public accommodation.

Ms. Burg: I think public accommodations, but when you talk about *Brown*, that involves the education issue. So I'm not sure. But I think you're right. Certainly it's not anything anyone talks about any more. When it comes to that extent, maybe it's hopeful that some day abortion will reach that point too. But I think that something else will have to come up to take its place. I don't know what that something else is going to be.

Ms. Rogers: Civil liberties and national security.

Ms. Burg: Now that's a scary area. But there the Patriot Act did not pass.

Ms. Rogers: It's definitely had an impact.

Ms. Burg: At least there are some members of Congress or the Senate at least who are willing to stand up against their party and that's a hopeful sign.

Ms. Rogers: Over the course of your career, do you think that anti-Semitism or sexism has had the bigger impact on your progress.

Ms. Burg: I think sexism. I didn't meet that much anti-Semitism professionally. Maybe because when I practiced law, not all but a high number of my clients were Jewish builders because in Washington that was the group that needed tax advice. On the bench, I certainly saw some of it at times. Both my sexism and my religion were used by disgruntled parties. I received some very nasty types of letters which attacked me for being a woman and being Jewish. I was told--I don't remember if I mentioned this in our earlier interviews--I was at the top of the list for what was a trial judge appointment for the old Court of Claims.

Ms. Rogers: Oh yes, you did say that. That was in the 70's and it was somebody who had explicitly called you Jew.

Ms. Burg: I don't whether he said it because I was Jewish or whether he said it just as a way of describing who I was, because people who knew him said that they did not believe it. Whether that was true or not or I really

Ms. Rogers: I think when you said it to me last time you said "Jew girl" or something like that. So it was a two-fer.

Ms. Burg: "That Jew girl will never get it as long as I have anything say to about it." And he had a lot to say about it. Both in that court and in the administration. So it was hard to say. But I think it was more my sex than it was my religion. There were a lot of Jewish judges.

Ms. Rogers: Oh certainly, you're right it might have been a code. I'm going to stop for one second. Okay, let's take a different path. Tell me a little about the considerations that you led up to your decision to retire and what you've been doing since.

Ms. Burg: I guess there were a number of considerations. One of them was that I did want to have a little more flexibility with my time and I think that if we had had a way of taking senior status, I would have seriously considered doing that. That's not true in the administrative judiciary. There has been talk about doing it at times but it has never been provided so that was not an option that was open to me. I wanted a little more time to do some of the things that I was interested in doing. Spending more time with grandchildren, and things of that sort.

Ms. Rogers: How long had you been there?

Ms. Burg: 22 years.

Ms. Rogers: And what year is this?

Ms. Burg: This is 1995.

Ms. Burg: And so, it was a time when alternative dispute resolution was becoming much more widely used,- judging in effect. I think a lot of the cases that we were involved in should and could have been resolved using ADR [alternative disputes resolution]. Actually now, at least at the Armed Services Board. they have picked that up and they are doing it and there are some of the judges that are doing a marvelous job of it, to the point that if I'm approached by some parties in dispute where the government is on one side of it, my first question always is why don't you go there because it's a freebie. Because to me there are some of the judges there who are just marvelous at it. But at the time I was there, we were not doing ADR, but it was something that always interested me. So I thought it was something I could be doing. This is essentially where the considerations are.

Ms. Rogers: And did you immediately start freelancing or did you give yourself some time off?

Ms. Burg: No, I immediately started freelancing.

Ms. Rogers: And are you affiliated with one of those groups?

Ms. Burg: Just with Triple A, but that's more. . . I don't get anything from them which is a big issue.

Ms. Rogers: In other words, they don't refer you any work?

Ms. Burg: Very little. I think there's politics involved, I'm sure. I'm on their list because the president of the organization or the executive vice president, now the executive vice president, at the time he asked me to do it because of something else I was doing before I retired. I had chaired a committee which was a joint committee. It started out through the American Bar

Association and was a joint committee of Triple A S, the American Association for the Advancement of Science, and the American Bar Association, where they had a joint committee dealing with scientific, technological and legal issues, and I chaired a subcommittee on the use of expert witnesses in the courtroom using court appointed experts so that you didn't have someone on either side saying one side or the other. There are some scientists, some doctors who are unwilling to appear for one party or the other but would be perfectly willing to appear at the request of a judge. So we did have a wonderful group which I chaired on the use of expert witnesses. The *Daubert* decision, *William Daubert, et ux., etc., et al., v. Merrell Dow Pharmaceuticals, Inc.*, 509 U.S. 579, is what is available to a judge in terms of accepting expert science testimony. Does it have to be something that's within the realm of scientific, where on the bell curve does itoccur?

Ms. Rogers: In terms of certainty, you mean?

Ms. Burg: No, not necessarily in terms of certainty, but in terms of, it's so far out of view, scientifically it's so far out, do you have to accept that testimony or does there have to be some basis for that presentation to be acceptable? I call it where on the bell curve that view exists. A judge has discretion under *Daubert, supra*,, a Supreme Court decision, to limit scientific evidence but it is primarily scientific background. Anyway this was a very interesting thing and when we began to develop a test program, I asked for a co-chair. From that I was asked by a person who had been involved in this as a recorder if I would join Triple A and I did and then they established a list of complex dispute experts. This creates a question of which came first, the chicken or the egg. This area vice president will not put you on that list until you've done 15 complex arbitrations under Triple A.

Ms. Rogers: So how do you get those?

Ms. Burg: So I had done some as a matter of fact but the way I have done them is because I have been asked personally by parties to be an arbitrator and to chair the arbitration panel and then because I'm on the list, they will do the administration.

Ms. Rogers: But it does count towards their...

Ms. Burg: Well it does count but I don't think I'll live that long. Because most of the ones I do are not through Triple A and this, you talk to most to people on the list and they have the same answer. And I am sure it's highly political.

Ms. Rogers: So that means it's 20 years since you've been with the government?

Ms. Burg: No, I retired in 95, did I say 85?

Ms. Rogers: In 95. Ten years. And has your level of activity waned much since then?

Ms. Burg: You mean.

Ms. Rogers: Doing your private work.

Ms. Burg: No it's very episodic. Sometimes I'm extremely busy and other times, I'm not busy at all.

Ms. Rogers: Do you have much control over it?

Ms. Burg: Only to the extent that if I am asked to do something and it's at a time I want to do something personal and the first time this happened, my husband said well we can rearrange our schedule, and I said I retired so I could do these things. So normally I will turn it down or they are willing to, if they really want me to do it, they will change the timing, so it fluctuates. Sometimes I am extremely busy, other times, I am not. Most of what I do is with prime and subcontractors. Some of it is private, some of it is where a subcontractor has a contract where the prime contract is with a government agency. Especially in mediations, I used to think that everyone wanted a neutral evaluation and now I've come to realize that's not true, that sometimes they just want a facilitator but if they come to me, they want a neutral evaluation. A mediation is so different from an arbitration. It's really a business decision in mediation. It's an entirely different way of looking at something.

Ms. Rogers: Do you do both?

Ms. Burg: I do both. I like mediations more.

Ms. Rogers: And these are all in that general subject area?

Ms. Burg: They're generally contracts. I've done some private contracts that have nothing whatsoever to do with public contracting but if I do private in most instances, they're in the construction area.

Ms. Rogers: And are these generally cases where there's a binding arbitration clause in the contract?

Ms. Burg: Not necessarily, because some of them for example, I did one where I chaired the panel, a very major case several years ago in Texas. Texas State was a party to it. And they had the same clause we have in federal but its not binding. My first question and the first question the other arbitrators all asked was." Why are you spending all this money to do a nonbinding arbitration?" And the answer was that they had purposely selected people who would be considered prestigious enough with the state legislature, because the legislature was involved indirectly with this, and that they wanted to, they felt that if we came out with a decision, that it would be so independent that they would leave it that way. And that's exactly what happened.

Actually, what happened is that we never went through the whole thing which was what we had hoped. We made segmental decisions and after several of them, the rest of them were all settled.

Ms. Rogers: And are most of the parties not so much the parties, the lawyers who come before you in this private part of your career. Are they men, primarily?

Ms. Burg: The majority, yes. But there are some women. There are several here in town in the construction area. Very prominent. One of the problems that I face and I don't know how one gets around this is that I am told by many people, when these things are done, they are done by lists, presented to both sides and both sides have to agree, and if the government is involved in a case I am turned down. Some of the government people, because of some of the decisions I issued, felt that my decisions were anti-government -- pro-contractor. Not the case. I mean that I feel that it's a very unfair accusation because the majority of my decisions were actually in favor of the government but there were some very major decisions that I issued that are still known, especially in the cost area which was indirect costs and things of this type, where they were bitterly resented even when some of them went up on appeal and were sustained on appeal, but in their opinion it was still, it was my fault. And I think that underlying a great deal of it was a basic, whether they wanted to accept it or not, a basic sex issue. Because these decisions went back many, many years early on. Two reasons, one I think because I was a woman who issued them and the other one with my background, I did not have Department of Defense. I was involved primarily, with the Department of Defense, but I did not have Department of Defense background. I was not an employee ever at any time with the Department of Defense. I came in, from the Atomic Energy Commission actually, but before that had been private, so I was not one of the boys or one of the gang. Because there are decisions that some of my colleagues issued that were far, far more objected to by the government--you know where they felt very strongly.

People feel different degrees of how strongly they feel about a particular issue. And these are all so arcane I wouldn't even begin to go into some of them with you. But some of them have been issued by some of my colleagues were far, far more adverse to the government position than I, but they were by men and they were by people who had at some point in their lives had had connection with the Department of Defense. But once a reputation, you know, as I had an instance recently where somebody called me and they had tried to have me mediate a case and it had been turned down and it was by the Navy and I know the chief trial attorney of the Navy who is no longer there. This is several years ago and as a matter of fact, he speaks on a panel that I chair every year at an annual meeting. I called him. And I said asked him what is this about. Yes, it's true, this young kid I don't think was born at the time of the decision that the Navy still holds against me. But, so you just live with this. When I talked before about what you need in terms of a judicial temperament. You cannot take these things personally and I had set a goal that I wanted to meet each year in my mind before I retired. I have more than met that goal every year and

Ms. Rogers: In terms of hours, income?

Ms. Burg: In terms of hours and income; hours are tied to income because I am paid by the hour.

Ms. Rogers: So how much would you say you're working over all?

Ms. Burg: 30 percent of my time, something like that. I'm talking about paid time. I am still very active in the American Bar Association, primarily in the Public Contract Law section. I co-chair a committee which has developed general procurement principles. A group of them have been adopted by the House of Delegates. I stay in the background, and am called upon for advice on occasion. This year was the 40th anniversary of the Public Contract Law Section .and we had a luncheon where they honored the pioneers of the section and it was an honor that I was one of them. And pictures of each pioneer was put up on the screen. All of the men were in their suits with their ties and mine was me holding a fishing rod, in my waders and holding up my fish.....

Ms. Rogers: Yes, I was going to ask you about that. Talk to me about fishing and why it is so important in your life.

Ms. Burg: Well it's important in my life because it's very important in my husband's life. It's the one way he relaxes. He leads a very intense life doing medical research and it's his real way of relaxing. Sure he reads, and we go to the opera, and we go to various things. There was a period in his life where he did woodworking. I don't know if you noticed the grandfather's clock. He carved and made it. There are things which he did. He does gorgeous work. Hasn't done any of it since PCs came in and he got interested in computers and programming. But his main way of relaxing is to fish and so I learned the hard way that if I wanted to really enjoy vacations with him I should become an angler. Oh sure, we go some places at times, primarily if he's invited to speak. We just spent two weeks in Scandinavia because he spoke. So we had time to relax a little bit, but his main way of relaxing is to go out to fish. And to do wilderness camping. I have friends that are absolutely shocked because I enjoy that kind of thing because before I met and married Moe my life when I went on vacation was the best room in the best hotel in the best city. They are shocked to think that I would enjoy wilderness camping. But it's different. I mean I still like the best room in the best hotel. But I also love to get out into the wilderness where you are away from everything. We haven't done that in a number of years because about 17 years ago we built a home in Montana and it's near a lot of fishing areas so we go there whenever we can in the spring or the fall. We don't go in the winter though some of our kids do. It can go to 50 below there and that's not my cup of tea. Anyway when we used to do wilderness camping every year, the chairman of the Armed Services Board who was also a fly fisherman, would go out with me before we went up and I'd get a little spinning backpacking rod which somehow always managed to "disappear" before we got where we were going and nothing else disappeared but that disappeared. So I took the hint and learned to fly fish. And I love it. The joy of getting out and standing in a stream as you're casting a line, watching for a fish. I don't really care if I catch fish though it's thrilling to get them on the line. I'm not a good athlete so to the degree this is a sport, no one else is dependent on my ability but you're alone, just you and world, and in beautiful surroundings. Not many people though some areas in this country have become so popular that there are lots of people but still you have your own space and you're just in your own world. It's utter relaxation and the pleasure of being out there. I remember being in Yellowstone National Park in the snow casting for fish and off in the background seeing a geyser erupt. It was just the highlight of my year. And so while its lovely to get to DC to see some of the museums and sights, it still does not quite compare to getting to the beauty of being in a special place alone with your fishing rod and relaxing in all its glory..

Ms. Rogers: Have you done it in other countries as well?

Ms. Burg: Oh yes, we've done it in New Zealand. About 15 times. This year instead of going to New Zealand we are going back to Chile where we have been previously. We are going down to Patagonia. There are lodges down there. And this one is new and in the real wilderness you can only get there by boat. You don't have any connections by telephone, no connections of e-mail, and for the first time in a long time we will not see e-mail for two weeks and I guess we'll survive. This particular lodge is two hours from nowhere but a very small town and it is owned by a civil engineer who is Chilean and I think comes from what one would call the high-level society. I have met his mother from Santiago. His wife is Australian. They met skiing in Switzerland one time. They have an alpaca farm so when you wake up in the morning, you might see an alpaca nose sticking against your window. The lodge has a beautiful central building and some smaller buildings on the stream that runs through their property that is so loaded with trout that it can almost become boring to catch them. They are all built out of the native stone and just lovely.

Ms. Rogers: So that's soon.

Ms. Burg: Yes, we're going the 6th of January. We will be there for two weeks, there for one week and we will be at their other lodge called the Dragonfly which we've not been to but I have heard great reports because of the pristine waters so this is the second year of its existence.

Ms. Rogers: Do you see yourself ever really retiring completely?

Ms. Burg: I don't know. Certainly, not at long as my husband continues doing research at NIH [National Institutes of Health]. My husband and I, we used to say when I retire, you'll retire, but I don't see him retiring at all as long as his health permits.

Ms. Rogers: Does he still work full-time?

Ms. Burg: Oh he works very full-time. He was a laboratory chief at NIH, is world-renowned, as I think I told you, a member of the National Academy of Sciences. He stepped down as lab chief several years ago. He had always kept his own section in the laboratory and done research even when he was chief. So one of his former fellows is now lab chief. As long as his health permits, he won't retire. I realized that years ago. It's such an important part of his life and he will just not retire and as long as he doesn't retire, as long as my health permits, I will certainly want to continue doing what I'm doing. I think it keeps the gray cells alive. I find it stimulating, exhilarating. If I'm at home I might get tired and want to take a nap in the afternoon. If I am involved in a mediation or arbitration I'm always amazed at how quickly the day disappears. I mean I do things with my time. I've gone back to taking piano lessons. I am involved to a little extent with organizations and have thought now that I can walk again with my new knees that maybe in the spring when we get back from our trip to Chile and, well maybe -- In March is my 80th birthday and my husband's 75th, so as our birthday party we are taking the whole family to Costa Rica. So maybe before then, maybe when I get back, it might be good to get involved in some volunteer work which I haven't had time to do for years. I do a little of it with the Susan Komen Foundation for the Race for the Cure. I may get involved with tutoring at some of the schools or something. I manage to keep very busy but I think as long as one's health permits, you should keep active.

Ms. Rogers: I think the fact that he works full-time is probably a bigmotivator.

Ms. Burg: So as far as working is concerned.

Ms. Rogers: You've got your own activities.

Ms. Burg: I think if he was not working, I don't know what we would do. I don't know that we would travel much more. Maybe spend the whole summers in Montana. That would be lovely. Other than that, I don't know what it would be like. Not to say we don't have some aches and pains but we do fairly well.

Ms. Rogers: Do you think with your children. I was thinking about this professionally. But I guess it's also true or can be as a mother, that you have more expectations or you're harder on your girls than your boys.

Ms. Burg: Oh definitely, that's a favorite thesis of mine. I was talking to one of my daughters about it yesterday because she was saying sometimes she feels she lacks emotion. She has a dog, now she has to decide what to do because he has developed cancer of the bone. What is the best thing for the dog? And sometimes she wonders if she's not emotional. So we got into a discussion which I've had with a number of people about expectations that strong and successful women have for their children and how this is reflected in their raising of their children. By strong, I do not mean physically strong, so maybe capable, intelligent and highly motivated are better words. I am a strong woman. I probably had more expectations of my daughters than of my sons. The truth is I have two very successful daughters. I mean they are mature women at this point who have done well with their lives and done what they wanted with them. One has been a homebody until recently. She has a great home. She was very active in the PTA in the days that you don't have many women like her involved in PTA work. Most of them are employed rather than doing volunteer work. Now that her children are grown, she has now returned to the working world and is a massage therapist – a far different field than her original degree in graphic art. The other one is an emergency room physician. They have tried to balance their lives with children. My sons are not as strong. I recognize that. I worry about them much more. Maybe I always have and maybe I've coddled them too much. I think a woman tends to do that more with sons. I've seen a number of instances where women who have both sons and daughters, it is the daughters who are stronger. It's interesting that you ask that.

Ms. Rogers: Well, as I've said, the funny thing is I was thinking about asking it with respect to treating litigants or colleagues or clerks or other people in your professional life, do you treat women any differently from men. And I partly say this because as I've told you I have daughter who's in the process of becoming a doctor and who has said often that the female residents and the female attendings treat the female med students tougher. So I was sort of wondering.

Ms. Burg: I think that if I wanted to be very honest, the answer is yes. And I've tried to guard against it. And I think I have successfully guarded against it. I have a number of men I have mentored also, who are not so young any more. One of whom you might know is Steve Schooner, a professor at George Washington University who has made the news in a lot of instances about government procurement and what should be done with it. And they're as complimentary to me and thanking to me, so I don't think I've done it exclusively but I at times have thought maybe, yes, that I have been tougher on women appearing before me. I do not mean to be but maybe expect more of them or want them to be successful since their actions reflect not only on them but on women as a whole.

Ms. Rogers: Work harder and be better.

Ms. Burg: To be better. Work harder. No I expect them all to work harder. Maybe it's not even be better. It's to recognize what they are trying to achieve and to be willing to really work at it and there I think I expect it equally of both men and women.

Ms. Rogers: I have one more question and you can do what you want with. It can either be a big discussion or a very little one. And that is, what observations if any do you have about women lawyers now and what opportunities they have or what they are doing to take advantage of them? How long a way we've really come. And things like that.

Ms. Burg: When I speak to young women's groups, and I still do at times these days, I guess my thesis is, we've come a long way baby, but we have a long way to go. I'm delighted at the fact that women have seen many things made available to them or they've earned the availability of them over the years. I think it is easier than it was when it was I got started. You still have to achieve, you've got to work at it. There is more of an old girls network now than there was. I think there have been changes but I think it is still harder. I think there are still problems. Women are still considered the homemakers, the mothers. Whether they consider it or not, they are faced with the problems of the maternal instinct, if you want to call it that, of raising of your children with a balance but without the sense of guilt that many of us have as we are trying to do many different things. The fact that there are more women in the law schools, 50%. You see more women getting ahead who are really good candidates. I think to that extent time will be helping in the 21st century. We have a long way to go in this century so one would hope we might see a woman President. I think in that respect it's different. I think it's easier for a woman to retain aspects of feminism now. She will still dress professionally, but I think the way one dresses professionally has changed. You don't have to imitate the men any longer. And I think there are more men who are willing to accept women as equals. I don't know if that resentment will ever change. I used to think it would but I am not so sure. You talk about your daughter in medical school. When my daughter went to medical school and this was of course was about 25 years ago, I don't know if they still have the same sport lecturers where an orthopedic surgeon would come in with all sorts of really anti-feminine remarks, etc. At this lecture she went up and told him exactly what she thought. And the class split down the middle, there was still many more men than women in the class, but it turned out the men in the class split. Those who were supporting her position and those that felt she was being silly. Or even stronger words. So I don't think that that has changed completely and I don't know that it ever will. We have to get to an Amazonian society. The dominant factor to have it. I don't have it. I heard yesterday or the other day, I heard that some of the women in Iraq were not voting and their husbands were voting for them. Obviously, they were afraid to go out to the polls in some areas.

Ms. Rogers: There's practical implications there though.

Ms. Burg: So it's hard to have… anyway.

Ms. Rogers: No, I said you could take it anywhere you wanted to go.

Ms. Burg: Things are easier. I was at a meeting the other day, a luncheon meeting the other day because, I had received the Bea Rosenberg Award and then once you receive it you're on the committee to help, not select, you don't select, you recommend to the president of the D.C. Bar who you feel should be the recipient. I would have loved to work in the tax section but they weren't hiring women. It's no longer true. Far from it. The Department of Justice has many women attorneys, because frankly they are willing to work for less money. I think what you find is that's true of all of the fields in the government that I had any dealings with, that many young men and women would go into the government for the experience which would always stand them in good stead when they would go out to the private sector. If they were very good, the private sector would gobble them up as soon as possible and offer far larger salaries than they could make remaining in the government. If you do trial work in the government, you are not working less hard than you would in private practice so the good ones are often skimmed off almost immediately, but women, many of whom were either as good or better than the men, nowadays I guess they are gobbled up as fast as the men, but earlier on were not. Or were more interested in maybe not working in the litigation end of it so that they could have more flexibility with their schedule. Times have changed in 50 years. Certainly, that's a radical change. And I think it essentially gets back to what I said when I started out, we've come a long way but there's still a long way to go. I think if someone like Harriet Miers did become chair of her law firm, there has to be ability there… It happens in corporations also but not as much. There are a few women general counsel of major corporations. Neither would have been the case 50 years ago.

Ms. Rogers: It's been one of the last barriers, I think. Women attaining leadership in a corporation.

Ms. Burg: Right now, the National Association for Women Judges is proud of how many women judges they have who are chief justices. But I think that's going to change. I haven't had a chance to discuss it with anyone but I think what we are seeing, since lot of those are based on the time that you served on the bench, these are a lot of the Carter appointees who have attained seniority. Carter made a very definite effort to get women onto the bench and probably more than more recently. I saw some study in the *American Judicature* that the Clinton administration, certainly the Republican administrations, there are not as many women as men appointed.

Ms. Rogers: Actually, I think the dip down was in the Reagan administration and then it started going back up a little bit in the first George Bush and then Clinton's was a big bump up and now.

Ms. Burg: Not as many as Carter's I don't think.

Ms. Rogers: Well, the, I think the percentage was at least as much.

Ms. Burg: That could well be. So I think that what you are saying was achieved in the federal…

Ms. Rogers: Had a lot to do with tenure.

Ms. Burg: I haven't sat down and really looked at it from that aspect. But I suspect that's what it is. But I think we will see it again and I think in time it will level itself off.

Ms. Rogers: So after all these hours of talking about your life and career and society, do you have any thoughts of things that we haven't covered that you would like to talk about.

Ms. Burg: It's been an interesting experience for me to kind of be introspective to look back over what has happened. I guess I'm grateful to people who have helped me. Many of whom were men. Most of whom were men.

Ms. Rogers: Well they would have to be then, I guess.

Ms. Burg: And the, I'm grateful for the fact that people who know me professionally still do respect me and like me. So I think it's possible to have both. And I've made some friends over the years in the various areas. So for all those things I am grateful. I just want to say, I'm happy with my life. I hope I have made a contribution. I hope I can continue to contribute and I hope that as the years go on, we'll see more and more women who are capable of achieving and being successful.

Ms. Rogers: Do you feel a great commitment to bringing women along in your particular area of the law?

Ms. Burg: Yes, oh yes.

Ms. Rogers: I presume it's still a pretty long haul in your area of the law.

Ms. Burg: Not as much as it was. We have more women involved in this section. We have more women in leadership positions of the section. We've had a number of women in the last few years. We have women on the Council. We have women who are becoming partners in the law firms. So that I see it as a very positive thing. But you still have, certainly in the military end of it, the admirals and the generals who have a certain hesitancy where women are concerned that they cloak in all sorts of different excuses but I think it all boils down to how they view women.

Ms. Rogers: Yes. You know it's one of the things that sort of interested me about your career that you chose almost from the get-go a lot of the areas that women weren't in and when I was starting law school or considering law school, I think a lot of people thought women do estates and trusts. And women do divorces and there are certain other things that women weren't really thought of particularly as litigators at that point and I know a lot of terrific litigators who are women but what we're used to seeing was this sort of tracking that was going on. And you've completely resisted that, it sounds like.

Ms. Burg: Because I've never looked at it that way. I think I've told you my parents raised us to feel we could achieve whatever we wanted to achieve and I think part of it was serendipity that this, but it never occurred to me that because I was a woman I had to stick within certain areas or certain confines. As a matter of fact, I fought against it.

Ms. Rogers: Well right, I think there was a consciousness there.

Ms. Burg: So I really feel that there my parents to a great extent deserve the credit for being way ahead of their time. I ended up involved in the Department of Defense. That was strictly happenstance. But it never occurred to me that I shouldn't do it because I was a woman. Or that I was going to have problems because I was a woman. To that extent I had sufficient self-assurance to feel that this was something I could do.

Ms. Rogers: Well on that note, I think that's a perfect note. I want to thank you on behalf of the Commission on Women for doing these interviews and it has been a real great education for me.

Ms. Burg: Well I want to thank you for giving me the opportunity of selecting me to do it. Because I think I do have a little story to tell so hopefully it might help other women along the way.

Ms. Rogers: I hope so. Thank you.

Ms. Burg: Thank you.